THE NEW AGE CHRONICLES

Vol 1, No 01 — A REL-MAR McConnell Media Company Publication — Digital Version - June/July 2018

Is "The New Age" Old News?

by Gwilda Wiyaka
Editor-in-chief

Many consider the New Age Movement to have its roots in a range of spiritual or religious beliefs and practices that developed in Western nations during the 1970s – just at the end of the "Commune Movement" of the 60s. Yet the Cosmic Humanist movement has its roots as far back as the Romantic poets of the 1800s. Ralph Waldo Emerson, Walt Whitman, and Henry David Thoreau rejected the God of the Bible, writing about a transcendent quality of spirituality experienced entirely through personal introspection.

In the late 19th century, Russian spiritualist Helena Blavatsky (1831 -1891) announced a coming New Age. She believed that theosophists should assist the evolution of the human race and prepare to cooperate with one of the "Ascended Masters of the Great White Brotherhood," whose arrival was imminent. Blavatsky believed the members of this mystical brotherhood to be the hidden world leaders who guided the destiny of the planet. Her ideas contributed to the concept of a New Age heralded by the coming of the Aquarian Age, that promised a period of brotherhood and enlightenment.

In the 1940s, Alice A. Bailey, founder of the Arcane School, suggested that a new messiah, the Master Maitreya, would appear in the last quarter of the 20th century. Bailey brought people together in groups of three to meditate daily, believing that they received divine energy, which they shared with others, thereby raising overall spiritual awareness.

After Bailey's death, other groups formed, claiming the ability to transmit spiritual energy to the world, and allegedly received channeled messages from various preternatural beings, such as the Ascended Masters of the Great White Brotherhood.

In the 1960s, the leader of the Universal Foundation, Anthony Brooke, traveled widely, predicting an apocalyptic event during the Christmas season of 1967.

In 1970, American theosophist David Spangler brought forth the idea that there would be a release of new waves of spiritual energy, as a result of astrological changes when the earth moved into a new cycle characterized by the Age of Aquarius. Spangler felt these events would initiate the coming of the New Age. He further suggested that people use this new energy to make manifest the New Age (i).

Eventually, the New Age movement lost its original focus of personal introspection and the evolution of the human race promised by the impending high frequency Aquarian Age. It became a catchall for doomsday theories, self-proclaimed channels, chrystal healing practices, and anything else that didn't agree with mainstream science and religion.

By the end of the 1980s, the New Age movement lost its momentum. Although viewed as a religious movement, it was disparaged for its acceptance of unscientific ideas and practices.

Following was the hype and hysteria about the Mayan calendar and the purported end of the world on 12-21-12.

Yet here we are, the Age of Aquarius is indeed upon us, and with it, monumental change and upheaval. While many of the early so called New Age beliefs were laced with giant leaps of illogic and faulty conclusions, the rapid transformative changes of our current times cannot be denied.

(Continued on Page 3)

Letter From The Editor

The New Age Chronicles

A REL-MAR McConnell Media Company Publication
ISBN: 978-1-927758-67-0 | ISBN: 978-1-927758-68-7

In This Edition of
The New Age Chronicles, No. 1, Vol. 1
June / July 2018

Page 01: Is "New Age" Old News - Gwilda Wiyaka
Page 02: Letter From The Editor - Gwilda Wiyaka
Page 04: Listen To Love - Corinne Zupko
Page 05: Negative Emotions Affect Your Health - Nauman Naeem
Page 06: DNA Is Not Your Destiny - Dawson Church
Page 07: Preventing And Reversing Diabetes - Pankaj Vij
Page 08: Frequencies Change Your Life - Ellen McDonough
Page 09: Cleansing And Dharma - Jonathan Glass, M.Ac
Page 10: Holistic Cancer Foundation - Carl O Helvie
Page 11: You Are At Risk: Autoimmune Disease - Kristin Grayce
Page 12: High Vibrational In The New Organic - Stephen Sinatra
Page 14: Intuitive Energy Healing - Wendy De Rosa
Page 15: Shamanic Parenting - Imelda Almqvist
Page 16: You Can Beat Cancer - Carl O Helvie
Page 17: Steve Judd's Monthly Musing - Steve Judd
Page 18: Our Advertisers
Page 19: Our Advertisers
Page 20: Optimizing Spinal Surgery- David Hanscom
Page 21: Gran's Garden - Gwilda Wiyaka
Page 22: A Voice Saved My Life - Bill Bennett
Page 23: Optimizing Your Intuitive Skills - Diane Brandon
Page 24: Intuition And Premonitions - Dawson Church
Page 25: Soul Retrieval and EMDR - Edie Stone
Page 27: Dreamtime And Shamanism - Sandra Corcoran
Page 28: Caves Of Power - Sergio Magaña
Page 29: On-line Shamanic Courses - Gwilda Wiyaka
Page 30: So, We're Still Here. Now What?- Gwilda Wikaya
Page 31: Courage To Tell Our Stories - Diana Raab
Page 32: Living Creatively With Nature - Kirby Hancock
Page 33: Find Your Path Home - Gwilda Wiyaka
Page 35: Transform The Past - Maureen Higgins
Page 36: Silence And The Unitive Experience - Christina Donnell
Page 37: Resonance - Cody Alexander
Page 38: SimulTV

DISCLAIMER: The opinions expressed in The New Age Chronicles Newspaper are those of the author(s) and do not reflect the opinions of REL-MAR McConnell Media Company or its Editors.

Information contained in our published works have been obtained by REL-MAR McConnell Media Company from sources believed to be reliable. However, neither REL-MAR McConnell Media Company nor its authors guarantees the accuracy or completeness of any information published herein and neither REL-MAR McConnell media Company nor its authors shall be responsible for any errors, omissions, or claims for damages, including exemplary damages, arising out of use, inability to use, or with regard to the accuracy or sufficiency of the information contained in REL-MAR McConnell Media Company publications.

Neither the editors, authors, publisher, or any other party associated with the production of REL-MAR McConnell Media Company published works accept responsibility for any accident or injury resulting from the use of materials contained herein. All persons who wish to engage in health / or mental health activities / alternative health regiments and/or suggestions, actual or implied, should receive professional medical consultation be commencement.

REL-MAR McConnell Media Company publications do not constitute legal, medical, or other professional advice. Information in REL-MAR McConnell Media Company publications is current as of the date of the printing.

The New Age Chronicles is © REL-MAR McConnell Media Company. All rights reserved. No part of any REL-MAR McConnell Media Company published work may be reproduced, stored in a retrieval system, or transmitted in any form or by any means, electronic, mechanical, photocopying, recording, or otherwise, without written permission from the publisher.

Rob McConnell, Publisher, REL-MAR McConnell Media Company, Hamilton, Ontario, Canada, L8W 3G9. Tel: (905) 575-1222, (800) 610-7035 Ext. 143, www.rel-mar.com, admin@rel-mar.com.

Letter from the Editor

Gwilda Wiyaka
Editor-in-chief

Myths, legends, prophecies and shamanic teachings across the globe have pointed to the time in which we are currently living as one of great transformation and strife – a time when old ways and systems fail, and a new order, or age, begins.

There has been much misinterpretation, hype, and hysteria as to what this really means. Many belief systems have appeared, ranging from: the end of the physical world, massive solar flares destroying all technology, a gigantic asteroid blowing us to bits, aliens landing and taking us away, reptiles taking over the world, to Jesus riding in on a cloud to gather the devout, leaving the sinners to perish. The list goes on, but suffice it to say, what is needed is the voice of reason within all the misinformation, illogic and chaos currently swirling around us.

There is no denying we are in times of transformation. As with all things in transition from one system to another, there is a period of chaos as the old way disintegrates, freeing the constituent parts to form the new.

And so it is, as the sun continues on its cyclic journey around the Milky Way, leaving the frequency represented by the Piscean age and entering the higher frequency area of the galaxy represented by the Aquarian age – the new age.

"Everything is energy and that's all there is to it. Match the frequency of the reality you want, and you cannot help but get that reality. It can be no other way. This is not Philosophy, this is Physics." ~ Albert Einstein

As we shift from the frequency supporting our prior reality and pass through a time of chaos, all the rules are changing. The higher frequency Aquarian age brings more luminosity, or light, by which to see. With it comes greater spiritual awareness and ever deepening levels of understanding. As we undergo this awakening, each person according to their gifts, willingness and intent, we may find we need tools to maintain balance in the chaos. As old rules and truths shift, we need the means to make sense of evolving realities.

The New Age Chronicles is a publication dedicated to providing the latest information and support, as we all transition into the new age.

Gwilda Wiyaka
Editor-In-Chief
The New Age Chronicles
editor@newagechronicles.com

Is "The New Age" Old News?

Continued from Page 1

What is really going on?

Dr. Aleskey Dmitriev is a professor of geology and mineralogy, the chief scientific member of the United Institute of Geology, Geophysics and Mineralogy within the Siberian department of the Russian Academy of Sciences, and an expert on global ecology.

Dmitriev's study cites that changes in the basic physics and behaviors of the Earth are becoming irreversible. There is strong evidence these changes are caused by our movement into what Dmitriev calls "a highly charged material and energetic non-uniformity" – or, in other words, a higher density energy in interstellar space.

This highly charged energetic material is being absorbed into the interplanetary area of our Solar System, creating what Dmitriev refers to as "hybrid processes and excited energy states in all planets, as well as the Sun."

Dmitriev also stresses is that this is not just his own hypothesis:

"A greater number of specialists in climatology, geophysics, planetophysics and heliophysics are tending towards a cosmic causative sequence version for what is happening. Indeed, events of the last decade give strong evidence of unusually significant heliospheric and planetophysical transformations."

Dmitriev also proposes the changes are forcing a more highly integrated view of the Cosmos.

"The climatic and biosphere processes here on Earth (through a tightly connected feedback system) are directly impacted by, and linked back to, the general overall transformational processes taking place in our Solar System. We must begin to organize our attention and thinking to understand that climatic changes on Earth are only one part, or link, in a whole chain of events taking place in the Heliosphere."

One of Dmitriev's major concerns is the effect that these changes will have on all life forms on Earth. Dmitriev concludes these changes could lead to a spontaneous mass evolution of humanity, creating "new and deeper qualities of life."

"The adaptive responses of the biosphere, and humanity, to these new conditions may lead to a total global revision of the range of species and life on Earth. New and deeper qualities of life may come forth, bringing the new physical state of the Earth into an equilibrium.

The current period of transformation is transient, and the transition of life's representatives to the future may take place only after a deep evaluation of what it will take to comply with these new Earthly biospheric conditions …

"Therefore, it is not only the climate that is becoming new, but we as human beings are experiencing a global change in the vital processes of living organisms, or life itself; which is yet another link in the total process."

The astrological ages, as well as the Mayan calendar, are actually a mapping of the solar system's cyclic relative positioning in the galaxy, in relationship to other heavenly bodies as well as energetic influences. It would appear Dr. Dmitriev's studies are observing the effect of the energy present in the portion of the galaxy characterized by the astrological Age of Aquarius, which mysteriously correlates to the end of the "end of days," foretold by the Mayan calendar.

While many mistakenly assumed this to be a literal foretelling of the end of the world, the Mayan calendar remains the most accurate calendar known to humankind. What if, instead of the end of the world, the Mayan calendar mapped the end of one era of frequency influence, and the beginning of another?

This would line up not only with the astrological prediction of the Age of Aquarius, but Dr. Dmitriev's scientific observations.

Unable to sleep in the wee hours of the morning, I bundled up in a blanket and sat on my porch. I live high in the Colorado Rocky Mountains, far away from any neighbors or light pollution. The moon had set and it was so completely dark, I couldn't make out the landscape at all. The only light was the morning star, shining like a diamond in the east.

Gradually, so slowly I couldn't perceive it changing, the sky shifted from jet black to dark indigo, silhouetting the pinion pines. Soon, I could make out details such as my porch railing, as the light slowly increased. I sat there for the longest time, marveling at the gradual transformation, until it became so light, the morning star disappeared. Yet at no time was I able to observe the process of changing. Finally, dawn broke as the sun predictably rose over the mountains.

It wasn't an earth shattering event, but a gentle emergence – a transformation that ended the night, bringing with it the light of day. However, I could not say precisely when the shift occurred.

Just so, we enter the dawning of a new age, and with it, a complete transformation.

We haven't been abducted by aliens, eaten by reptiles, nuked by atomics, struck by an asteroid, carried off by angels, or blown up by the sun. So, we're still here. Now what?

What we need is a voice of reason in these tumultuous times.

What is required is a new approach to the New Age, one backed by science and reason. We need leading edge, well researched information on these changing influences, in order to chart our way.

Indeed, let's start anew, sans the hype, hysteria and untrained, self-proclaimed gurus who have appropriated from a plethora of ancient practices, while having little to no understanding of their original form or application.

At the same time, we need not throw out the baby with the bath water. The changes we are experiencing are cyclic. In one form or another, we have been here before and will be here again. Hidden in many ancient practices are viable tools, developed during our last pass, that can now ease our way. Let us immerse ourselves in serious study of what has been left, as well as the new scientific facts emerging.

The New Age is not old news – it is upon us. Much like the sunrise, it is gradually emerging, bringing with it massive, profound and lasting change. Let's regroup, reframe, rethink and endeavor to evolve gracefully.[]

www.missionevolution.org

Listen To Love

Choosing to Listen to the Voice of Love in Times of Fear

Corinne Zupko, Ed.S., L.P.C.,

Wherever we look, there appears to be endless cause for anxiety. It seems natural, even easy to be fearful, while peacefulness seems elusive, reserved for some time in the future.

This fear can wear on our bodies and minds. But worse, the fear compounds itself. As we give energy to one fearful thought or belief, our thoughts multiply with other reasons to be afraid, causing us to limit what we do, robbing us of sleep and leaving our coping mechanisms ineffectual.

This was my life — overwhelmed by constant anxiety, afraid of what was going to happen next, worried sick about health and the well-being of loved ones. Today, things are different. I sleep well, wake up with peace in my mind, and feel a sense of ease throughout the day. What happened? This shift gradually came about as I started to listen to the voice of love in my mind, instead of the voice of fear. It took ongoing practice and commitment.

The voice of fear is what we are accustomed to. It tells us that everyone else has it better, we aren't worthy or "lucky," shouldn't bother trying, that we'll be happy only when we achieve a certain goal like the perfect job, the perfect partner, etc. Yet, if we get any of those things, we find ourselves fearful of losing them or wanting something else. The voice of fear, which is the source of strain, fuels dissatisfaction, conflict, and division.

The opposite is the voice of love, telling us of our joy, our safety, and worthiness. It brings forth a sense of ease. It tells us that everything we could possibly need is found within us, right now. But...the voice of love is quiet, easily drowned out by the voice of fear.

Herein lies our problem. There is nothing in our culture that consistently encourages us to stop, slow down, and choose again. Instead, the voice of fear is actively reinforced by the world, and because it is so loud, choosing love can seem impossible. Yet, it is more than possible to do so.

To practice choosing love in times of fear, experiment with these steps:

1. Make Peace Your Goal.
You want a peaceful mind, but it is important not to tie your peace to a specific outcome, like staying on your diet, for example. This desire for peace is always the first step in choosing to listen to the voice of love. Decide you want to learn how to consciously respond to challenging circumstances with love, rather than having knee-jerk reactions based on fear.

2. Know That Love Is In You.
Even though the voice of fear is loud, there is part of your mind that knows how to perceive with love. Through your willingness to acknowledge and turn to the quiet part of your mind that knows love, you give space for loving perception to return.

3. Be Willing To See Another's Challenging Behavior as a Call For Love.
When triggered by another person's words or actions, can you be willing to see their behavior as a call for love? If someone is causing pain, it must be because they are in pain themselves, and don't recognize that they are listening to the voice of fear.

4. Get Honest.
There are areas in our lives where we'd rather judge and condemn. If you do not want to perceive with love, that's okay, but be honest with yourself about this. Leave a tiny bit of willingness that there might be another way of perceiving a situation. What would it hurt to ask the part of your mind that is loving to see things differently? You don't have to actually see with love, you just have to be willing to see in order for a shift to come.

5. Practice Putting the Loving Part of Your Mind In Charge.
I once tried to send love to everyone I passed on a 5-mile walk. By the end, I was exhausted. The next time, I simply turned to the part of my mind that knows love and said, "I am willing to see with love. Show me the way." Encouraged by the 5-mile-high feeling of gratitude that spontaneously occurred for everyone who passed by, the experience remained with me as a touchstone for further practice.

Perceiving with love is not condoning or approving the actions of another, but rather it is about opening your heart to join with the love that exists in all of us. This is crucial because in this world, what is seen by one as loving, another may see as hurtful. A powerful prayer I have used to help me open up to seeing with love is, "I want to see the love in you, because I want to know it in myself." If love is truly what we are made of, then I can come to know it in myself by my willingness to see it in others.

About the Author: Corinne Zupko, EdS, LPC, is the author of From Anxiety to Love. As a licensed counselor and keynote speaker, she has helped thousands of individuals through her one-on-one counseling, weekly meditation classes for corporations, and the largest virtual conference of ACIM in the world through the organization Miracle Share International, which she cofounded. She lives in New Jersey. Visit her online at www.FromAnxietytoLove.com. []

THE 'X' ZONE BROADCAST NETWORK
Broadcasting 24/7/365
For The Very Best Of
Paranormal, Parapsychology,
New Age and Much More!

- A Different Perspective with *Col. Kevin Randle*
- Connecting with Coincidence with *Dr. Bernie Beitman, MD*
- Eureka Radio Show with *Glenda Shenkal*
- International Police Association Radio Show with *Les Bodrogi*
- Kal's Korner with *Kal Korff*
- Know the Name with *Sharon Lynne Wyeth*
- Mission: Evolution with *Gwilda Wiyaka*
- Paranormal StakeOut with *Larry Lawson*
- Seek Reality Radio Show with *Roberta Grimes*
- Two Good To Be True with *Justina Marsh and Peter Marsh*
- The 'X' Zone Radio Show with *Rob McConnell*

www.XZBN.net

a Div. of REL-MAR McConnell Media Company

Negative Emotions Affect Your Health?

Is There a Link Between Negative Emotions and Disease?

Dr. Nauman Naeem, MD, FCCP, FRCPC

Do negative emotions affect your health?

Conditions such as depression and anxiety have been shown to affect how we manage and treat our other chronic conditions, but even if one does not suffer from these conditions, unresolved emotions can pave the way for chronic diseases to manifest. These unresolved emotions include grief, anger, jealousy, hatred, guilt and shame, to name a few. Now I am not saying that there is anything wrong with experiencing these emotions. What I am saying is that when these emotions are not allowed to percolate through our being but are repressed and ignored, emotional blocks can arise, leading to physical symptoms which eventually manifest as illness. But how does one know if they have emotional blocks?

Emotional blocks can be identified by situations in our lives where we get triggered and have intense negative feelings which keep us from handling the situation effectively. Usually, the situations that trigger these emotions are similar to emotionally traumatic, or similar distressing situations that we have experienced in the past in our infancy, childhood and early adolescence.

For example, if we were left to cry in the crib frequently when we were seeking attention and physical touch, this could be interpreted as abandonment by the subconscious mind. Similar situations in our adult life could trigger those same feelings, such as being stood up on a date. There are many experiences we have when we are young which, if not processed emotionally, can lead to issues later in life. These do not have to be major emotionally traumatic events, such as physical or sexual abuse. They could be subtle and unrecognizable by those around us. For example, if, as a child, your sibling was offered a treat such as ice cream and you weren't, this could be interpreted as neglect, even if this was not your parent's intention. If the parent does not recognize their child's interpretation of this event as neglect, it will be ignored by the parent and perpetuate the feeling of neglect in the child's viewpoint.

Most children do not have the courage or the maturity to confront such feelings to see if there is any external validation for them, in which case they become lodged in the subconscious mind. In our example, the feeling of neglect will be translated as unworthiness by the child and can affect his or her future experiences, such as whether he or she applies to the university of his or her choice, strives to obtain the job he or she desires, or pursues his or her lifelong dream or ambition. Sooner or later, the feelings of neglect and unworthiness can result in depression and physical symptoms, which can manifest as illness.

How do these negative feelings lead to illness?

Suppressed negative emotions lead to chronic stress, which leads to overstimulation of the adrenal glands with an increase in cortisol release. Over time, the adrenal glands will burnout, leading to a decrease in cortisol secretion, so-called adrenal fatigue. This will result in a decrease in the anti-inflammatory effect of cortisol, with rampant inflammation, eventually leading to chronic disease.

So how does one prevent this from happening?

Like I mentioned before, the problem is not the negative emotions themselves, as we are all bound to experience these at various points in our lives. The problem is not allowing ourselves to experience them fully and allow them to pass right through us.

The truth is that we are multi-dimensional beings, mental, emotional, vibrational and spiritual, who take on a physical form for our journey here on earth. Our physical form, here on earth, has to and will experience the full spectrum of human emotion, which is needed to experience our-selves as whole beings, including the so-called negative emotions or the shadow self. It is only through the full human experience that we can know ourselves as whole.

The problem is that negative emotions are often too painful to bear and we block and suppress them, which results in chronic disease as I have already described. The main driving force for suppressing these emotions is fear of pain. However, our fears are often unwarranted. There are two types of fear – psychological fear and actual fear. Actual fear registers a real danger to our lives, such as encountering a jaguar in the jungle. Psychological fear is from those circumstances, conditions and feelings which our ego tells us will bring us pain.

The problem is that the ego is only looking out for its own sustainability, with no thought of our greater growth and development. Therefore, it often keeps us stuck in old paradigms and ways of thinking and being which keep us from growing, which can only happen when we lean outside our comfort zones. One of the ways we can lean outside our comfort zones is to not resist our negative emotions, and allow ourselves to experience them fully and completely. If we do this, we will realize that the feeling is simply our soul's experience of a specific moment in the physical body and not to be feared, as all feelings, at their core, lead us to inner peace and unconditional love. We can then gain clarity about what action we need to take in our lives to deal with the situation which led to the negative emotion. This is how negative emotions can be transmuted and fuel our journey to experiencing our higher consciousness, which is our true nature. This is how we can also prevent negative emotions from leading to chronic stress and, eventually, to chronic disease.

Here is a case study to illustrate this point. I had a patient, whom I will call Lisa, who came to me for shortness of breath and chest pain. She had multiple investigations, including a CT scan of her chest, which showed inflammation in her lungs and lymph nodes. I did a bronchoscopy, which is a test where I take a long flexible device with a camera and a light to go into her lungs and do a biopsy. This did not reveal any specific diagnosis and her symptoms persisted. I eventu-ally referred her to a thoracic surgeon for a lung biopsy.

Before this happened, she had planned a vacation to Trinidad, where she is originally from. While she was there, her symptoms had, miraculously, completely disappeared, but when she got back, they returned. I then started to question her further about stresses in her life. It was then that she revealed to me her marriage was not working, and there was a lot of tension and conflict with her husband, who had not gone with her on the trip.

This was proof that her symptoms were a direct result of her grief over her failing marriage, be-cause when she was away from him for some time, her symptoms resolved. She did not require much convincing that her symptoms were related to the grief and stress caused by her husband, and she resolved to leave the situation immediately.

Can you recall a time when negative emotions derailed your health? Are you still suffering from the effects of unresolved emotions? I hope you now have more insight into the nature and meaning of emotions, and how they can fuel and enhance your life's journey.

If you would like to learn more about this and similar topics, please visit www.naumannaeem.com

About the Author: Dr. Nauman Naeem, MD, FCCP, FRCPC is a pulmonary and critical care specialist. During the course of his career, spanning two countries and caring for tens of thousands of chronically and critically ill patients, he noticed the majority of patients do not heal, remaining trapped in the paradigm of chronic disease. This led to exploring the roots of true healing through studying ancient healing traditions and the psychology of healing, consciousness and metaphysics, culminating in his book, Healing From The Inside Out. He continues his medical practice in Ontario, Canada, bridging conventional medicine with a more holistic, multi-dimensional approach to healing. His website: www.naumannaeem.com []

The International Police Association Radio Show with Les Bodrogi
www.iparadioshow.net

D.N.A. Is Not Your Destiny

Your DNA is Not Your Destiny

Dawson Church

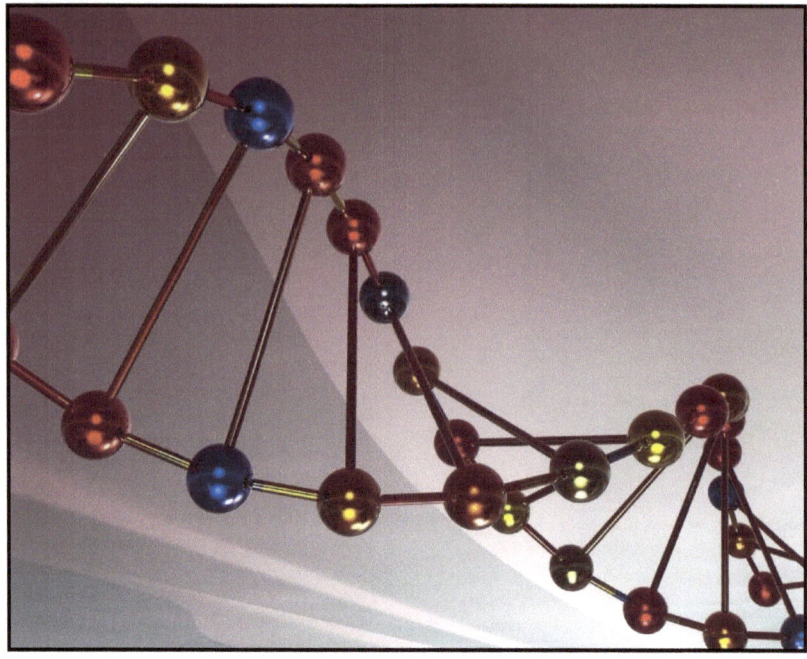

One of the most fascinating and newest fields in science is epigenetics. Epigenetics measures changes in DNA that are due to influences outside the genes themselves. I've been involved in many studies of epigenetics, and its effects since the turn of the century.

Just because your cells contain a gene doesn't mean it's active. Genes need to be turned on, or "expressed," in order to have an effect. It's like turning on a light: the switch must be tripped in order for the light to shine. Simply having a gene doesn't mean it's expressed any more than simply having a bulb means that the light is turned on.

In particular, I study the epigenetics of stress. Genes that contain the genetic code for stress hormones, like cortisol and adrenaline, are turned on by stress. Stress triggers the expression of these genes, and your body uses that genetic code to build the hormones themselves. Stress > gene expression > hormones.

In my book Mind to Matter: The Astonishing Science Behind How Your Brain Creates Material Reality, I tell the story of Janice, a friend of mine who was diagnosed with breast cancer. At first, she panicked. Gene tests showed that cancer genes, called "oncogenes," were highly expressed in her cells. Like lights, they were turned on.

I urged Janice to do everything in her power to reduce her stress levels, knowing that this would dial down the expression of the genes that code for cortisol and other stress markers that are typically higher in cancer patients (Balkwill & Mantovani, 2012).

Janice quickly got serious about healing. She phoned or emailed friends in the medical and research worlds, as well as experts in energy medicine. She began to use a variety of energy methods to center herself daily. Those included qigong, meditation, and EFT tapping. EFT (Emotional Freedom Techniques) uses fingertip tapping on acupuncture points, in combination with affirmations. Over 100 studies show that it's highly effective for anxiety, depression, and stress (Church, 2013). Meditation and qigong also have hundreds of studies supporting their efficacy for both physical and mental illness (Jahnke et al., 2010; Goyal et al., 2014).

Three months later, after changing her energy and her attitude 180 degrees, and consistently practicing these methods, Janice went back to the hospital for another comprehensive battery of tests. Her new diagnosis? "Cancer free." Her oncogenes were no longer expressed. Janice had shifted her energy and consciousness, and the genes of her body had shifted in response.

Albert Einstein said that, "The field is the sole governing agency of the particle." Energy fields like those that doctors measure, using medical devices like MRIs and EEGs, shape the particles of which our bodies are composed.

We aren't used to thinking of energy techniques like meditation, tapping and qigong as "real" medical interventions, like pills and surgery. Yet research shows that they profoundly change our bodies. When we reduce our stress levels in this way, we change our consciousness. That can flip the switches that determine which genes are turned on. In a study of veterans with PTSD who received 10 sessions of EFT, my colleagues and I found that 6 key genes were switched on, including genes that reduce inflammation throughout the body (Church et al., 2018).

Your DNA is not your destiny. Your genes do not determine your future, any more than having bulbs in your home determines whether or not the lights are on. As you deliberately choose to shift your consciousness, calming your stress, filling your mind with positive thoughts, and regulating your field with energy techniques, you turn on the lights of healing and regeneration throughout your body.

Dawson Church is the author of Mind to Matter: The Astonishing Science of How Your Brain Creates Material Reality. He has conducted many scientific studies of health and epigenetics. He shares scientific breakthroughs on gene expression and peak performance at DawsonGift.com.

His website: https://dawsonchurch.com/

References:

- Balkwill, F. R., & Mantovani, A. (2012). Cancer-related inflammation: common themes and therapeutic opportunities. Seminars in Cancer Biology 22(1), 33-40. Academic Press.
- Church, D. (2013). Clinical EFT as an evidence-based practice for the treatment of psychological and physiological conditions. Psychology, 4(08), 645.
- Church, D., Yount, G., Rachlin, K., Fox, L., & Nelms, J. (2018). Epigenetic Effects of PTSD Remediation in Veterans Using Clinical Emotional Freedom Techniques: A Randomized Controlled Pilot Study. American Journal of Health Promotion, 32(1), 112-122.
- Goyal, M., Singh, S., Sibinga, E. M., Gould, N. F., Rowland-Seymour, A., Sharma, R., ... & Ranasinghe, P. D. (2014). Meditation programs for psychological stress and well-being: a systematic review and meta-analysis. JAMA Internal Medicine, 174(3), 357-368.
- Jahnke, R., Larkey, L., Rogers, C., Etnier, J., & Lin, F. (2010). A comprehensive review of health benefits of qigong and tai chi. American Journal of Health Promotion, 24(6), e1-e25.[]

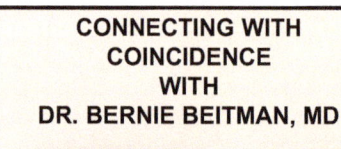

CONNECTING WITH COINCIDENCE WITH DR. BERNIE BEITMAN, MD

From Coincidences to Synchronicities - Take the Test!

www.coincider.com

Preventing and Reversing Diabetes

Six Lifestyle Choices For Preventing and Reversing Diabetes

Dr. Pankaj Vij, MD, FACP

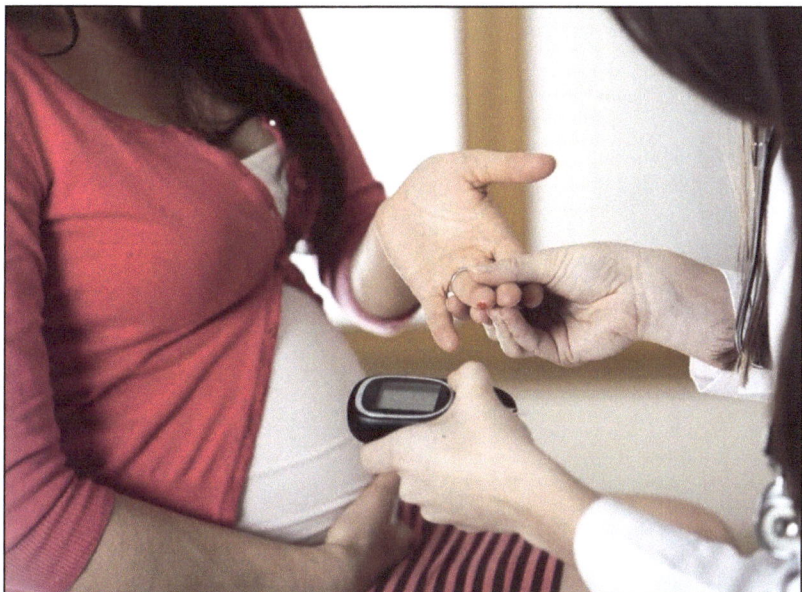

The ancient Greek physician, Aretaeus of Cappadocia (c. 81—c. 138), described diabetes as a "melting down of the flesh and limbs into urine."

Many experts argue that type 2 diabetes is an incurable disease that gets worse with the passage of time. As a matter of fact, this is what is taught in every medical textbook: Type 2 diabetes is a gradually progressive chronic disease that affects all the organ systems of the body. It can be managed but not reversed.

But new research raises the tantalizing possibility that drastic changes in lifestyle may reverse the disease in some people. As it turns out, type 2 diabetes is the direct result of an accumulation of visceral fat, or belly fat, in the midsection of the body. Studies have also shown that obese individuals who have bariatric surgery frequently see the condition vanish, long before they lose any weight at all, suggesting that metabolic diseases are a result of hormonal imbalance, which can be corrected.

We know that type 2 diabetes is caused by insulin resistance resulting from droplets of fat blocking the insulin receptors on the liver, the muscles, and in all the tissues that require insulin to open the channels for glucose to enter as a fuel. Therefore, if we can figure out a way to remove the fat blocking the insulin receptors, it makes sense that we could reverse this condition.

At the turns out, type 2 diabetes, as well as obesity, high blood pressure, and cardiovascular disease, all of which are disorders of metabolism, are to a huge extent, the result of our lifestyle choices. That means that by fixing the lifestyle choices that created insulin resistance, we can prevent and often reverse these metabolic diseases.

The key to using lifestyle as therapy is to first understand, and optimize, the master levers of health. While there is a lot of controversy, even among experts, about the best diet, there is absolutely no controversy about the following six master levers of health.

When we optimize six master levers of health, we can create conditions for the body to return to its default state of balance, harmony and wellbeing, effectively reversing metabolic diseases and losing fat in the areas where it needs to be lost.

1. Eat a Nutrient Dense Plant Rich Diet.
Eating foods that you would encounter in nature generally provide the healthiest nutritional value. If you must buy packaged foods, carefully read the ingredient labels and pick the ones with the fewest ingredients. Drop juices, sodas, artificial sweeteners and chemical additives. Drink water as your main fluid and steer clear of dairy and alcohol.

2. Make physical activity inevitable.
We are made to be in constant motion. Start a weight-resistance program and make a commitment to 10,000 steps every day. You can walk or run in place, on a treadmill, in a mall, on the trails, or just around. Just get it done. Evidence in the research has demonstrated that walking at least 10,000 steps every day has the greatest return for effort in improvement in overall health maintenance for exercise.

3. Quit Smoking. Period, enough said.
Also eliminate chemical toxins, which have made their way into our food supply. Meat, eggs and dairy are a big source of toxins, and conventionally farmed produce can be harmful, too. Eat organic whenever possible.

4. Get Enough Sleep.
Our vital systems replenish, rejuvenate and reset themselves when we get deep restful sleep. Many of us are getting less than our required amount of sleep, wreaking havoc on our metabolism, appetite regulation, and immune system.

5. Manage Your Stress.
Activation of the parasympathetic nervous system with some form of meditation, whether it is concentrative, expressive, or mindfulness meditation, can act as an antidote to the constant onslaught of damage from modern living.

6. Enjoy Meaningful Social Connections.
Deep and meaningful connections with other people are vital to the maintenance of health. These are people we can discuss our innermost thoughts with, without feeling ashamed or judged. The benefits go far beyond psychosocial and extend into physical and mental aspects of our health. "Friend power" may be more important than willpower, because our social circle is a strong determinant of our lifestyle choices.

About the Author:
Pankaj Vij, MD, FACP, is the author of Turbo Metabolism. As a doctor of internal medicine, he has helped thousands of patients lose weight, manage chronic health conditions, and improve their physical fitness. Visit him online at http://www.doctorvij.com.

Based on the book Turbo Metabolism. Copyright ©2018 by Pankaj Vij, MD. []

THE 'X' CHRONICLES NEWSPAPER
The World's First
Paranormal / Parapsychology
Newspaper
Is Now Available
With Our Compliments
at
www.xchroniclesnewspaper.com

Published monthly since 1990, The 'X' Chronicles Newspaper, is read and downloaded in over

7,238

Identified Cities
Around The World

Stories and articles include topics such as - UFOs, Ghosts, Hauntings, Demonic Possession, Alien Abductions, Government Conspiracies, Psychic Phenomena, Remote Viewing, Bigfoot, Urban Legends, Near-Death Experiences, Ancient Mysteries, Unsolved Mysteries and so much more, all in one place, in one publication...

www.xchroniclesnewspaper.com
A div. of REL-MAR McConnell Media Company

8 Frequencies Can Change Your Life

How Healing Frequencies Can Change Your Life

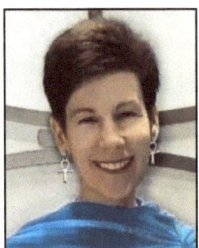

Ellen McDonough

Is it possible to improve, health, wealth, sleep, youthfulness, and achieve spiritual awakening through energetically-encoded audios? I believe it is.

In the mid-2000's, I suffered from terrible burnout, combined with extreme fatigue and a series of bizarre symptoms that no one could explain, let alone heal. While dietary changes and supplements helped the symptoms, they were not a cure. I saw countless health practitioners, both allopathic and holistic, but despite their best intentions, nothing changed. I felt miserable, depressed and hopeless.

Fortunately, synchronicity led me to discover audio tracks infused with powerful, high frequency energies and with specific, pure intentions. I was familiar with energy work like Reiki, but was skeptical that just listening to audio tracks could be effective; even so, I decided to give them a try.

To begin with, some of the audios triggered a detox; however, after a few days, I gradually began to feel better, as if some old energy that had been weighing me down had lifted.

After that, I decided to try other energetically-encoded audios that did everything from clearing chakras to shifting consciousness. Eventually, by listening to energetically-encoded audios from a number of different healers, one by one, my symptoms vanished and my energy returned. While this wasn't the only factor in my recovery, these audios, produced by healers around the world, played a key role.

What are Energetically-Encoded Audios?

Basically, an energetically-encoded audio is one that's been infused by a healer with powerful intentions and spiritual frequencies to create a specific, positive change in your life.

Some energetically-encoded audios include music, some include Light Language, others include talking, and some are completely silent. Some have binaural or other types of beats, which are known to affect your mental state and brain waves.

Once you have the audios, you can listen actively, or in many cases, simply loop the audio in the background during the day, or even while you are sleeping. The audios can last from a minute to an hour or longer.

Some examples of how energetically-encoded audios can help transform your life include:
- clearing your energy field
- expanding your consciousness
- clearing and aligning your chakras
- improving sleep
- increasing abundance
- rejuvenating and re-contouring your body

Since everything is composed of energy and vibrational patterns, by introducing high, spiritual energies carrying a specific intention, the current condition must shift to a more harmonious state. Virtually anything is possible with high spiritual frequencies!

Where Can You Get Energetically Encoded Audios?

As I began to connect with more people in the mind/body/spirit world, I found that not many knew about these unique audio experiences, but most were curious and wanted to give them a try.

It turns out that most of these audios are not available via iTunes. Currently, these are the choices for getting energetically-encoded audios:
- Tele-summits. Many of the healers who produce these types of audios are guests on tele-summits. They are interviewed by the host where they describe their work and offer special packages for a limited time, typically when they have new audios.
- Individual Healer Websites. Many of the healers have their own websites where you can buy and download individual audios or audio packages. You can download them to your computer or transfer them to your mobile phone. Mobile App. We recently created the PureLight Audio mobile app, which is a central marketplace for these audios, as well as instructions for how to use them. Many of the healers who offer energetically encoded audios have included their products and packages in the app, and many more will be added over time.

Price points for audios vary, but many healers have free tracks so that you can experience an energetically encoded audio for the first time.

It is my hope that these little known gems help others create positive changes in their own lives, just as I have in mine.

About the Author:

Ellen McDonough is the founder of PureLight Audio www.PureLightAudio.com , a mobile app available from the iTunes App Store.

Ellen is also a visionary artist who channels images of Atlantis, high spiritual realms and other star systems, then imbues her images with Light and high frequencies. Ellen's art may be viewed at www.PlacesofLight.com. []

NEW AGE QUOTES

- "The only time you fail is when you fall down and stay down." - Stephen Richards, Cosmic Ordering: You can be successful

- "If you want the best the world has to offer, offer the world your best." - Neale Donald Walsch

- "You don't need to change the world; you need to change yourself." - Miguel Ruiz

- "I've always hated the "Who are you?" question. This is a philosophical inquiry. Answering that question is why we're on earth. You can't answer it in thirty seconds or in an elevator." - Sandy Nathan, Numenon

- "I have a special pair of poop shoes under my desk. Whenever I need to drop a deuce, I slip them on and scurry to the restroom, and no one ever knows it's me. Like, if I'm wearing Louboutins that day, and my producer sees Earth shoes in the stall....well, you get the idea. It was truly a lightbulb moment when that came to me." - Oprah Winfrey

Cleansing and Dharma

Cleansing and Dharma: The Foundation of True Fulfillment

Jonathan Glass, M.Ac

Cleansing has been at the core of Ayurvedic medicine for thousands of years. Perhaps, now more than ever, due to high stress levels and an overabundance of environmental toxins, we would benefit from doing a cleanse twice each year.

When people think of cleansing, they often have images of fasting, colonics, gallbladder flushes and juicing. While these can all be components of effective cleansing, they are only aspects of Ayurvedic cleansing.

According to Ayurveda, cleansing includes not only the body, but the mind and soul as well. Its goal is improved physical wellbeing, along with a clearer mind and a renewed spirit!

Ayurveda teaches that human beings have five primary goals in life. Cleansing is meant to clarify and purify these goals within each of us so that we can live our lives at our greatest potential.

They are:
- Dharma: fulfilling our essential life purpose
- Artha: fulfilling our basic needs for survival
- Kama: fulfilling our need for pleasure
- Moksha: fulfilling our desire for freedom and spiritual liberation
- Prema: fulfilling our desire for pure, unconditional love (the love of God)

All of us have these same fundamental goals. While all the goals are important, dharma is the root of them all – and fulfilling our dharma is actually an essential goal of cleansing. The following material looks at the components of dharma and how we can fulfill it in our lives.

Dharma

We all desire to awaken to our full potential. To do so, we must live and act with integrity and according to our true nature. This is called dharma. We all have a dharma, or purpose, that perfectly suits us. Dharma sustains us and is the foundation for fulfilling all five goals of life.

Dharma is the predominant quality inherent in an object or person. For example, the dharma of fire is heat and light. Acting and working according to our dharma is essential for satisfaction.

Personal and spiritual growth begins with being your authentic self. Paraphrasing a verse from the Bhagavad Gita, "It is better to be yourself, imperfectly, than to try to be someone else, perfectly." We shine our own light better than anyone else can.

Dharma ultimately relates to our spiritual nature, or jaiva dharma, "the eternal function of the soul."

Dharma has four principal dimensions. They are:
- Satya: truth
- Saucha: purity
- Ahimsa: nonviolence (compassion)
- Tapas: discipline

The four dimensions are like four legs of a table. When all four legs are strong, the table will be stable, fulfilling its "dharmic function" as a table. If a leg is weak or missing, the table will wobble or collapse. For dharma to manifest, all four legs must be present.

Satya: Truth

The Sanskrit word for truth is satya, which means both "truth" and "ever-present existence." Truth is self-sustaining, existing on its own, without effort. It is being our authentic selves – sincerity at its best. It takes effort to manipulate an image of ourselves, but it is effortless to simply be ourselves. Truth, in all forms, has a health-sustaining influence. Creative self-expression is based on accepting our true nature, with its gifts and limitations – the challenge and gift of existing authentically. Both personal growth and spiritual growth are fully dependent on this first leg of dharma.

Saucha: Purity

The Sanskrit word for purity – internal and external cleanliness – is saucha. Purity is the power in us to discriminate between what is helpful for fulfilling our dharma and what is not. The process of digestion is a good example. When we eat, the small intestine extracts the nutrients and passes on the rest to be eliminated. Similarly, purity empowers us to accept those things that are truly beneficial and reject those that are not. Purity protects the heart (physical and spiritual) by letting go of that which is toxic to the body, mind, and soul and accepting that which serves our highest wellbeing.

Ahimsa: Nonviolence/Compassion

The Sanskrit word for nonviolence is ahimsa. It is the power of wise compassion and is the foundation of dharma. Nonviolence means restraining from taking action that causes emotional harm in any way, to humans, other living beings, the environment, or our self. Sometimes we forget that focusing on the faults in others is also harmful to ourselves, as we ingest the very same negative qualities that we perceive.

Real nonviolence leads to love and compassion—the higher purpose of nonviolence. Thus, authentic yoga traditions generally recommend a vegetarian diet--an important part of ahimsa.

Tapas: Discipline

The Sanskrit word for discipline is tapas. It means heat or friction. Tapas indicates the fire-like, focused intensity that burns through any obstacle to fulfilling our goals. Once we pass through this fire, like trials of adversity, we emerge brighter, clearer, and closer to attaining our purpose. Imbalanced discipline, ignoring the other legs of dharma: truth, purity, and compassion, is not dharma. Dharmic discipline means to act in alignment with these other principles. It takes discipline to eat well, work hard, and become successful. It also takes discipline to take time for fun, personal growth, supporting loved ones and choosing compassion over selfishness.

Discovering our dharma is an ongoing, lifelong process – it deepens and continues to reveal itself. Passion is an indication of our dharma.

To manifest our dharma, all four legs of dharma must be present. That takes time. Life has many teachers, whether they come as spiritual mentors, cleansing, or as life experiences. All are intended to gradually help us fulfill our dharma.

Cultivating all four legs in all we do liberates an internal source of energy and power, one beyond ordinary human functioning. When we fulfill the other four goals of life in the context of dharma, our life becomes peaceful, vibrant, successful, and happy. Regular cleansing always helps us to clarify our purpose in life, thus fulfilling our dharma!

About The Author:

Jonathan Glass, M.Ac, is the author of the Total Life Cleanse and the co-creator of the Total Life Cleanse program. He is a Master Acupuncturist, Ayurvedic Practitioner, herbalist and Natural Health Educator. Jonathan served on the faculty of the New England School of Acupuncture and The Dharma Institute of Yoga and Ayurveda. He has facilitated thousands of individuals through his group-supported, transformational cleanse programs, for over twenty years. Jonathan has been in private practice since 1987 when he co-founded the Healing Essence Center with his wife, Katherine, in Concord, Massachusetts.

His Website: www. totallifecleanse.com

Recipe for Love

Ingredients

- 2 Hearts Full of Love
- 2 Heaping Cups of Kindness
- 2 Armfuls of Gentleness
- 2 Cups of Friendship
- 2 Cups of Joy
- 2 Big Hearts Full of Forgiveness
- 1 Lifetime of Togetherness
- 2 Minds Full of Tenderness

Method

Stir daily with Happiness, Humor and Patience.

Serve with Warmth and Compassion, Respect and Loyalty.

Author: Unknown

Dr. Carl O Helvie
HOLISTC CANCER FOUNDATION

Meet Carl O Helvie, R.N., Dr.P.H., - Carl O Helvie, R.N., Dr.P.H. is a registered nurse with a doctorate in Public Health (Johns Hopkins) and over sixty years' experience as a nurse practitioner, educator, author and researcher. He has published 8 books and chapters in 4 additional ones, and published 40 articles, presented over 55 research papers internationally and 60 papers for lay groups. Some of his books resulted from his development and over 35 years refinement of the Helvie Energy Theory of Nursing and Health that has been used internationally in practice, education and research by 9 countries. Read more about Carl O Helvie at www.HolisticCancerFoundation.com and www.BeatLungCancer.com..

CARL O HELVIE HOLISTIC CANCER FOUNDATION

The Carl O Helvie Holistic Cancer Foundation differs from others because we focus on:

- A holistic approach
- Multiple aspects of education, research, patient care and politics
- Multiple cancer types

A holistic approach consists of combining physical, mental and spiritual modalities as well as considering the environment, relationships and politics because all of these elements influence health and wellness (cancer and recovery) and may need to be assessed and included in any treatment plan.

An important part of any cancer program is education for those who have cancer or want to prevent it as well as lawmakers who influence cancer programs and public access to these programs through the decisions they make. Likewise, because we evolve in a dynamic environment cancer causation changes over time and consequently ongoing research is needed to identify and find solutions to these changing causes. In today's world where harsh invasive drugs and procedures that often compromise the immune system have evolved as the treatment of choice for most medical conditions including cancer, medical coverage is often denied those who wish to find treatment outside the conventional realm. These cancer patients are subsequently often required and frequently unable to pay for their treatment of choice. This gap provides a rationale for both funding patient care and involvement in the political process to bring about necessary changes in cancer care and funding. Please visit and donate today!

www.HolisticCancerFoundation.com

Are You at Risk for an Autoimmune Disease?

Kristin Grayce McGary
LAc., MAc., CFMP®, CStcert, CLP

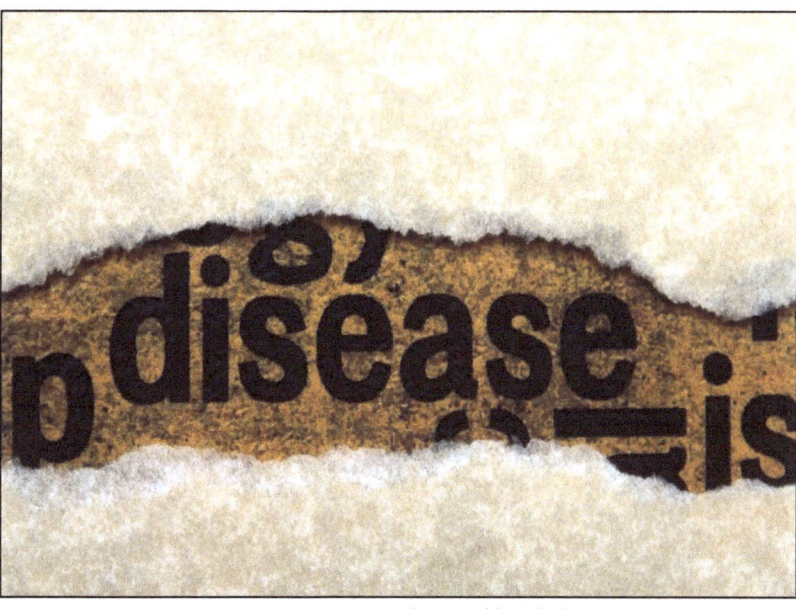

50 million Americans suffer from autoimmune diseases, costing almost 100 million dollars a year. It's a growing number. And while you may believe that you're healthy, eat well and "never get sick," you could have autoimmunity – a pre-diagnosable disease state.

Any autoimmune disease always begins with autoimmunity – where the body's immune response attacks healthy cells and tissues, glands and organs, eventually manifesting into a full-blown disease. Put simply, the body has misidentified a part of itself as a foreign invader and mistakenly attacks it.

According to John Hopkins University's Autoimmune Disease Research Center, autoimmune diseases are a special threat to women. Indeed, more than 75% of their patients are women.

Sadly, autoimmune diseases are among the ten leading causes of death among women in all age groups up to the age of 65.

I've had an autoimmune disease called Hoshimotos Thyroiditis. About 90% of all thyroid disorders are actually autoimmune issues, but they are left misdiagnosed or undiagnosed until such extensive damage is done to the thyroid gland that it's difficult to fully recover. I suffered for years before I discovered what was really going on. I needn't have suffered and I can help you to protect yourself from autoimmunity by passing along some of the knowledge I have accumulated.

Conventional medicine practiced in the West has few answers for those suffering from autoimmune issues and there's little sight of a cure. It has been my experience that autoimmunity and full-blown autoimmune diseases are symptoms of deeper issues.

Allopathic medicine tends to focus on relieving symptoms, rather than getting to the root cause of the problem. From my point of view, autoimmune issues, such as allergies, food sensitivities, digestive issues, foggy thinking, exhaustion, weight gain, repeated infections, even cancer, are red flags. Clearly, they point to a dysfunctional immune system. And that can lead to any one of a number of crippling autoimmune diseases, such as MS, rheumatoid arthritis and lupus.

"Never getting sick" may seem to you like a good thing. That you're doing OK. But it could very well be the complete opposite and a sign of an under active immune system – it may even be the beginning of an autoimmune disease. It takes a well-regulated, strong, and balanced immune system to create a fever and kill a bunch of bad bugs that have invaded your body. A fever is one of the most natural anti-cancer reactions your body can produce. It's a time when your white blood cells are ten-fold and they are kicking the butts of the invading viruses. In my view, the last thing you should do is suppress that fever with acetaminophen or ibuprofen. Fever suppressants shut off an important immune response and don't allow your body to do what it was designed to.

So how can you avoid an autoimmune disease or help your body to recover from one?

Fortunately, holistic and functional healthcare providers have developed approaches that get to the root of autoimmunity and autoimmune diseases, providing relief and remission. It usually begins with the gut. The gut is the throne of your immune function. About 75% of your immune system comes from your gut, which makes it essential to the functioning and balance of your immune system.

Remember I said that autoimmune issues can take years to fully manifest? This means your gut may be inflamed and out of sorts without you even knowing it, or you may dismiss symptoms that you attribute to aging that are actually a sign of a deeper issue. An autoimmune issue may be lurking and you won't even know it until it could be too late. Take note of allergies, food sensitivities, digestive issues, such as gas and bloating, constipation or diarrhea, fatigue, repeated infections or lack of fever; they could be warning signs of something more serious.

In my practice, I worked with a patient who had chronic joint inflammation and pain in the knees, shoulders and hands. She was also taking prescription thyroid medication but had never had a full thyroid panel (10 markers as opposed to the conventional standard of TSH, T3 and T4). I found it surprising that she had been prescribed a particular medication without a detailed analysis of the gland that the medication was supposed to be supporting. Furthermore, she had never had a truly comprehensive functional blood chemistry analysis which would shed light on any deeper medical issues. Her conventional doctors had been working blind.

I always want to see a full panel of tests. When I saw the results of this patient's tests, what we found was shocking. She'd been taking thyroid medication for at least 10 years and her thyroid antibodies were high. No one had ever bothered to test them or explain their importance to her. Once we were fully armed with the appropriate data, she began a gut repair nutritional and lifestyle program. Within weeks, her antibodies dropped, her joint pain vanished, and she reported clearer thinking. Not only was gut repair helping regulate her immune system, it was also helping support her brain. (The gut is commonly known as the Second Brain.)

In order to really know the degree of risk you're facing for autoimmunity or an autoimmune disease, I recommend a truly comprehensive lab panel that is interpreted by someone who understands how to look for the underlying root issues, and can individualize treatment based on your unique health and life expression.

Additionally, that health care provider must also be able to interpret your comprehensive lab results based on functional medical reference ranges, rather than their limited conventional counterparts. You are unique, and what works for you may not work for your best friend. It's necessary to get all the information and also have it properly interpreted, according to your individuality and health goals.

About the Author:

Kristin Grayce McGary LAc., MAc., CFMP®, CSTcert, CLP is a highly sought-after health and lifestyle alchemist. She is renowned for reversing annoying and debilitating health conditions and helping people to live with clarity and vitality. Kristin Grayce is also a speaker and author of Ketogenic Cure; Heal Your Gut, Heal Your Life. www.KristinMcGary.com []

THE 'X' ZONE BROADCAST NETWORK
The Very Best In
Pranormal, Parapsychology, New Age
Radio Programming
www.xzbn.net

High Vibrational Is the New Organic

High Vibrational Is the New Organic

Dr. Stephen Sinatra

There's a saying that "everything old is new again." We see it with art, fashion, design, and I personally see it play out time and again in the health world.

Take yoga, for example. It actually goes back to ancient India, yet only became popular in the West in the mid-20th century. It still took another 50 years for Westerners to see it as something everyone, not just contortionists and "free spirits," can do as part of a healthy lifestyle.

Organics and superfoods are two more great examples. Only recently has the idea of superfoods garnered mainstream attention, even though some have been celebrated since ancient times for their health benefits – olives and honey by the Greeks, and chia seeds by the Aztecs.

Organic food? It's as old as farming itself – but it didn't become a movement until recently, when people started to question all of the toxic, unnatural chemicals and GMOs creeping into our grocery stores.

Today, yet another example of this is emerging: high vibrational. I call it the "new organic." What's old is new again.

What Is a High Vibrational Lifestyle?

High vibrational is a way of life . . . like organic, it means "close to Nature." But high vibrational takes organic a step further by focusing on the energy of everything. Rocks, food, stars, trees, TVs, you, me – you name it – everything in the universe is made of vibrational energy, interactive subatomic particles; and everything we consume or surround ourselves with ultimately impacts our energy and health – for better or for worse.

The idea that everything is vibrational is not new. Energy was (and is) the theme underlying various holistic health philosophies in ancient Greece, India, and China. Here in the West, though, it took until the mid-20th century and Albert Einstein's Nobel Prize-winning theory, $E=mc2$, which described the interchangeability of mass and energy, to persuade us that energy and health could be linked. The theory actually proved that the "good vibes" and "bad vibes" we get from people, places, and things aren't just in our heads – we actually feel them in our bodies, at the cellular level.

Stay with me, here.

We generally think of the body as a "mass" of flesh, bone, and blood, but Einstein's theory tells us that the body is also a bundle of vibrating electromagnetic energy. And this is true. Every single cell in the body, whether it's in your brain or your big toe, vibrates at a microscopic frequency. There's a natural pulsation to its activity.

When cells are healthy, they're able to efficiently metabolize nutrients and make all the energy your body needs. Their vibrational frequency is higher than unhealthy cells. And your vibration is really the sum energy of all your cells.

Living a high vibrational lifestyle means living in a way that helps raise or maintain your body's natural vibrational frequency. Some of those choices will sound familiar, like eating fresh, whole, organic foods that promote strong cell metabolism – and avoiding things that don't, like cigarette smoke and other environmental toxins. But the real magic of high vibrational living lies in recognizing the energetic interconnectedness of everything in our world, and in learning how to combine all of those energies with our own feelings, intentions, and habits to increase our health and longevity.

It's organic taken to the next level: organic food, organic lifestyle, organic thinking and feeling – organic being.

How to Raise Your Vibration

To help you get started on a high vibrational path, here are the core principles I encourage people to follow:

1. Know Your Food's "Energy Chain"

Quick question: which sounds healthier? (A) a tomato that grows and ripens naturally under the warmth of the sun, or (B) a tomato that's doused in pesticides, picked while it's still green, and then exposed to ethylene gas, which forces it to turn red, ripe or not.

It's not much of a contest. This is a good illustration of what I call the "energy chain" in food production. Foods that are produced organically and as close as possible to the way Nature intended them to be, not only tend to have higher nutritional value, but they have a higher vibration because they include less of the bad stuff – like pesticides, preservatives, or other chemicals – that can damage cells in the body. They also carry in them the energy of the wind, sun, rain, and sea.

Go organic with food as much as you can, and try to make the majority of your diet plant foods. Steer clear of sugar and processed foods, which are usually loaded with vibration-lowering additives, preservatives, and artificial sweeteners.

As a bonus, most high vibrational fruits and vegetables are also rich in fiber, which helps your body naturally detox a lot of cell-damaging toxins. That's a win-win, if I've ever seen one!

2. Get Grounded

No, I don't mean confining yourself to your room. Quite the opposite, in fact – get outside! The Earth emits its own vibrational energy, which you can absorb through the bottoms of your feet. So take off your shoes and socks and go for a barefoot walk on your lawn, in a neighborhood park, or (my personal favorite) on the beach.

Earthing, or grounding as it's also called, literally reconnects you with Nature, while at the same time helping to rebalance some important parts of your physiology. It helps reset your autonomic nervous system, which helps you relax, sleep, and better manage stress. It's also a potent solution for stopping free-radical damage to cell membranes. Plus, with any trip outdoors, you're also getting a healthy dose of sunlight and fresh air.

If you can't get outside, don't worry. You can also connect with the Earth's healing energy by using an Earthing device.

(Continued on Page 13)

High Vibrational Is the New Organic

Continued from Page 12

3. Be Positive and Grateful, and Honor Your Feelings

If you want to live your best – and healthiest life – your heart and mind have to be partners, not enemies.

Emotionally, this means honoring your feelings. They are your truth and they deserve to be felt, even if they're negative. Anger, fear, hatred, grief, and jealousy may have a lower vibration than joy, love, and hope, but they are not as dangerous as denial. Whenever you "push down" and ignore an emotion, you bury a subconscious time bomb in your body. The constant stress of carrying around that negativity lowers your vibration, and may come back to you one day as pain, disease, or dysfunction.

Protect yourself by finding safe places to experience your emotions so you can let them go, and then re-energize with vibration-raising feelings of love, joy, gratitude and peace.

Intellectually, this means tuning into your thought patterns. Is your inner voice a critic or a cheerleader? Refueling your mind with positive thoughts can help you be more accepting, hopeful, and optimistic, which can help lower your stress level and raise your vibration.

When your heart and mind are attuned, you'll not only feel happier and healthier yourself, but you'll be a positive force in the lives of the people around you.

4. Channel Your Stress

Stress is one of the best examples of how Einstein's theories about energy and mass relate to health and well being.

When you have lots of stressful thoughts and feelings, and don't do anything to channel them, you literally embody the energy of stress. Headaches, tense or sore neck, shoulders or back, stomach upset, high blood pressure, and insomnia are just some of the physical symptoms you might experience. Some stress is good, but too much lowers your vibration and can rob you of your health.

How do you channel stress? You've got to let that energy flow – through your breath! Focused breathing is at the core of vibration-raising mind-body practices like yoga and meditation. Breathing deeply not only helps you set that stress energy free and balance your nervous system, it helps you deliver more vital oxygen to all the cells in your body so that they can make more energy!

The other key, of course, with yoga and meditation is letting go of your thoughts – the distractions of the mind – and just being in your body. . . honoring it for being a friend to you.

I also love regular moderate exercise for stress relief, since it also offers so many cardiovascular benefits. Making exercise fun is what will make it stick as a lifestyle habit.

Dance, uninhibited play with the kids or grandkids, and walking the dog are all great options – whatever does it for you.

As you can see, literally every aspect of our lives affects vibration – so it's easy to begin making changes that will improve yours. Just apply this one rule: When faced with a decision – whether it's about what to eat, what products to buy, or even what you want to do with your spare time – choose the "organic" option: the one that's as pure, natural, and true to who you are as possible. If you can do that, you'll be on your way to higher vibrational energy and better health.

About the Author:

Dr. Stephen Sinatra is a cardiologist, certified nutritionist, bioenergetic psychotherapist, and anti-aging physician. He is also an author of numerous books, and is founder of Heartmdinstitute.com, a health and wellness information site. He is also founder of Vervana.com, through which he provides healthy food for people, and AgelessPaws.com, where he offers all natural treats and supplements for pets.

References:
• Greenfield, RH. "Mediterranean Superfood: Olives." Doctor Oz. Dec. 14, 2011. www.doctoroz.com/article/mediterranean-superfood-olives
• Eptakili, T. "The Best Greek Superfoods." Greece Is Health. Jan. 6, 2017. http://www.greece-is.com/greek-superfoods/
• Trafton, A. "Chemical energy influences tiny vibrations of red blood cell membranes." Phys.Org. Dec. 21, 2009. www.sciencedaily.com/releases/2009/12/091222122025.htm
© 2017, 2018 Vervana. All rights reserved []

The Mandela Effect

About

The Mandela Effect refers to a phenomenon in which a large number of people share false memories of past events, referred to as confabulation in psychiatry. Some have speculated that the memories are caused by parallel universes spilling into our own, while others explain the phenomenon as a failure of collective memory.

Origin

In 2010, blogger Fiona Broome coined the term "Mandela Effect" to describe a collective false memory she discovered at the Dragon Con convention, where many others believed that former South African President Nelson Mandela died during his imprisonment in the 1980s. That year, Broome launched the site MandelaEffect.com to document various examples of the phenomenon.

See, I thought Nelson Mandela died in prison. I thought I remembered it clearly, complete with news clips of his funeral, the mourning in South Africa, some rioting in cities, and the heartfelt speech by his widow.

Then, I found out he was still alive.

Additionally, Broome described other widely held false memories, including various nonexistent Star Trek episodes and the death of the Reverend Billy Graham.

Spread

On August 23rd, 2012, a post titled "Berenstein Bears: We Are Living in Our Own Parallel Universe" was published on the blog The Wood Between Worlds,[2] which described a widespread memory of the children's book series Berenstein Bears as "Berenstain," explaining the false memory as the result of an alternate reality spilling over into our own. In December 2013, the /r/mandelaeffect[3] subreddit was launched for discussions about the phenomenon. On November 29th, 2014, the YouTube channel ShineTheLight73 uploaded a video titled "The Mandela Effect Exploded After The 2014-2015 Biblical Blood Moon Tetrad," which garnered upwards of 900,000 views and 2,200 comments over the next three years. []

Forrest Gump – Life IS like a box of chocolates, or Life WAS like a box of chocolates?

Fiona Broome

If you recall the famous line from the Forrest Gump movie, which of the following did Forrest say?
a. "Life was like a box of chocolates…"
b. "Life is like a box of chocolates…"
The answer in this reality is A: "Life was like a box of chocolates…"

In my original response to this issue, I said:

Forrest Gump's accent is fairly heavy, and he doesn't always enunciate clearly, but — the the film clip (https://youtu.be/CJh59vZ8ccc) — I hear "was" far more than "is."

Appeared in the 1994 film Forrest Gump, when the lead character Forrest Gump (played by Tom Hanks) says "Mama always said life was like a box of chocolates. You never know what you're gonna get." [Emphasis added.]

The book Norwegian Wood by Haruki Murakami, first published in Japanese in 1987, and in English in 1989, has the following: "Just remember, life is like a box of chocolates." … "You know, they've got these chocolate assortments, and you like some but you don't like others? And you eat all the ones you like, and the only ones left are the ones you don't like as much? I always think about that when something painful comes up. "Now I just have to polish these off, and everything'll be OK.' Life is a box of chocolates."

I'm not sure how much accent and enunciation, as well as pop culture references, have contributed to this apparent alternate memory. So, I can't say this is a Mandela Effect issue.

However, one-for-one, everyone I've asked in real life about this quotation has been 100% certain the line was "Life is like a box of chocolates…"

Is the Mandela Effect fact or fiction? You be the judge.

For more information on the Mandela Effect, visit www.mandelaeffect.com.

Intuitive Energy Healing

How to Clear Your Energy Blocks with Intuitive Energy Healing

Wendy De Rosa

Over the many years in my practice, I've had people say, "I feel blocked... I want to clear my blocks...." Or, "I want to release these blocks that keep me from feeling ____ (fill in the blank here)." Yet, what are energy blocks? Why do they affect us and how can you clear them with Intuitive Energy Healing?

What are energy blocks?

Energy blocks are imprints of life experiences stored in the energetic body during a time when the conscious was not able to process or repair the imprint. Similarly, not all blocks are negative. As an example, if a parent says to you at an early age, "Only trust mom and dad and don't trust anyone else," that belief becomes an imprint in the energetic system, usually in the Root Chakra. As a young toddler, it is important for the child to bond to safety and trust their parents, and have boundaries. Yet, as the child grows, this belief becomes a hindrance, because part of developing safety includes trusting others and trusting self. If the belief of only trusting mom and dad (which is fear based) doesn't get repaired by the parents offering a new belief and teaching, then this belief becomes a block.

Blocks can be old belief systems, stored and unprocessed emotions from a challenging experience, fear, or survival mechanisms from early family systems, but are outdated when living in the world.

Blocks are also subconscious, which means they are part of someone's operating system that gets acted out subconsciously, until a person becomes conscious of the pattern or block and decides to heal it.

How can you clear energy blocks with Intuitive Energy Healing?

First of all, there are many ways to unravel a block. I use the word "unravel" because there could be layers to the block, emotions about living without it and/or emotions surrounding it that were present at the time of life when the block formed, or even a purpose for why the block is there and how it was needed for a period of time.

Intuitive Energy Healing is a process of looking at an energy block from an intuitive perspective and applying breath and awareness to release the emotions and energy relating to the block. This would require tuning into the soul's voice or consciousness around why the block was there, where it came from and whether it is still needed. In order to do this, it would require working with someone who is an intuitive energy healer, OR tuning in to your own energy system and unravel the block.

Here is how you can unravel the block on your own:

1. Find a quiet space, free of distractions and take some deep breaths to get grounded in the space.
2. Ask yourself where you feel the block in your body? Let your body or your soul tell you.
3. Take some deep breaths into this area of your body.
4. Ask this block to tell you what it is, how long it has been there, who it came from, and what purpose it is serving you now. Even if it is negative, this serving you in some way.
5. Now tell the block you are ready to step into your light and your power and you no longer need the block. Tell the block it is free to go.
6. Breathe into any and all emotions – from here out – as you guide your breath to this area of your body to release it.
7. Release the block by letting it go down to the earth through a long grounding cord, or up to the heavens to release, or simply allow it to dissolve.
8. Thank the block, if needed, for getting you this far, and let it know you are going to step into your power now.
9. Feel your power, presence and light fill into the space, once you have released this energy of the block.
10. Declare: "I am free of this block and expanding into who I am here to be." Feel free to choose your own wording here.

Intuitive Energy Healing is a powerful way to release the feelings of stuck, irritable, angry, upset, lethargic, and more. These 10 steps will get you off to a great start on how to clear your energy blocks using intuitive energy healing. If you find you do need more help, or you would like to learn more about Intuitive Energy Healing, you may visit the schoolofintuitivestudies.com for further support.

About the Author:

Wendy De Rosa is international intuitive energy healer, speaker, teacher, and author. For the past two decades, she has offered private sessions, education and training programs for spiritual and personal growth for anyone wanting to develop their intuition, clear their blocks, and experience personal transformation. She is the founder of The School of Intuitive Studies and The Intuitive Healer Training Program. Wendy has filmed two programs for Mindvalley.com's spiritual growth channel Soulvana, and she is a faculty member of The Shift Network. She has appeared on CBS News/Better Connecticut four times and her book Energy Healing Through the Chakras: A Guide to Self-Healing is an Amazon Best-Seller. Wendy is also a contributing author to the Best-Selling book, Bouncing Back: Thriving in Changing Times with Wayne Dyer, Bryan Tracy, John Assaraf and other leaders in personal growth. Out now is Wendy's 3rd book, Expanding Your Heart: Awakening through Four Stages of a Spiritual Opening. []

Paranormal StakeOut with Larry Lawson
www.xzbn.net

Shamaic Parenting

Shamanic Parenting
Making Good Choices =
Making Spirit-led Choices

Imelda Almqvist

My first book, "Natural Born Shamans: A Spiritual Toolkit for Life (Using shamanism creatively with young people of all ages)," was published in August 2016. Since then, informally and in interviews, I have frequently been asked, "What makes shamanic parenting so different from 'regular parenting?'"

The key issue is that in shamanic parenting, the parent acknowledges the child has their own team of helping spirits, just as the parent does. This means there is a third presence (or voice) in the parent-child relationship – Spirit.

All parents want their children to do well, to make good choices. In the secular society of "mainstream 21st century parenting," this can become a battle of wills and opinions between child and parent as to what constitutes a good choice. Different generations can arrive at surprisingly different priorities and interpretations.

Shamanic parenting opens another option or pathway: you encourage your child to seek guidance from their helping spirits, while you consult with your own team. It may mean moving forward in a way that neither child nor parent has thought of before. It may also mean choosing a direction that does not feel safest or most secure – but will generally turn out to be the right choice long term.

Young children are "natural born shamans." They naturally talk to spirits, operate from magical consciousness and feel connected to All That Is. Traditional parenting and schooling often suppresses this. Children are put under pressure to conform to and operate within the scientific paradigm (with a Christian overlay), which Western culture presents as the dominant, and only, means of perceiving reality.

However, if we can encourage children to live from a strong connection to their own helping spirits, it removes some of their anxiety. Their team of allies is always with them, even in situations where we parents cannot follow. Their team will still be present, long after we leave the planet. Hopefully, they will pass the gift on to their own children and grandchildren. The most precious gift of shamanic parenting is a viable spiritual navigation system and spiritual compass, available to our children 24/7.

Shamanism acknowledges the importance of initiations and ordeals as major windows for soul making and personal growth.

Rather than shielding a child from pain and life's challenges (which comes naturally to all parents!), the shamanic parent will support a child through these periods, always delivering the message, "I know you can do this, but I am there for you!"

Some shamanic parents go one crucial step further and actively seek rites of passage for their child, because they are aware that many young people today are failing to step through critical developmental windows. Western culture has lost this ancient art, ignoring the sacred role elders of the community play in this process. Rites of passage and initiations prepare a young person for taking their place in the tribe as an adult. Generally, there is a strong focus on the young person meeting key spirit allies during this time of being tested, so the spiritual navigation system is fully "charged" with all "apps activated" (to use a modern metaphor).

Another important issue is that shamanic parents commit to walking their own healing journey, meaning they actively work on themselves facing their shadows and inner demons. This is a great gift to children, because in doing so, parents learn to separate "their own stuff" from "their children's stuff." It is comparable to the daily polishing of a mirror or window – parent and child can see each other's authentic selves and give one another space to live from their true expression.

This process can remove many layers where children carry the unlived dreams of parents as well as deeper ancestral issues. Young people become free to truly forge their own way in the world. They are less burdened by the choices and struggles of those who came before them, yet more able to achieve full expression of the talents and gifts they received from those same ancestors.

Carrying ancestral/emotional/spiritual burdens that belong to parents or ancestors is extremely common in children. The issue is not fully understood by many mainstream professionals when families ask for help. Shamanic healing work and family constellations work can cast light in this area and offer ways of healing.

It is my observation that shamanic parenting creates independent, empowered young people with a healthy sense of self and purpose, as well as parents who are able to protect and guide, yet willing to dance with the untried and unexpected.

If this path speaks to you and you want to know more – I invite you to read my book!

About the Author:

Imelda Almqvist is an international teacher of shamanism and sacred art. Her book Natural Born Shamans: A Spiritual Toolkit For Life (Using shamanism creatively with young people of all ages) was published by Moon Books in 2016. She is a presenter on the Shamanism Global Summit 2017 as well as on Year of Ceremony with Sounds True. She divides her time between the UK, Sweden and the US. Her second book Sacred Art: A Hollow Bone for Spirit (Where Art Meets Shamanism) will be published in December 2018.

Imelda's website: www.shaman-healer-painter.co.uk []

THE 'X' ZONE CHANNEL…
24 / 7 / 365

The Paranormal, Parapsychology, Unsolved Mysteries, Cryptozoology, Space Exploration, UFOs, Extraterrestrials, Ghosts, Hauntings, Psychic Phenomena, Conspiracy Theories, Bigfoot, Lake Monsters, The Bermuda Triangle and Much More!

Exclusively on SimulTV
www.simultv.com

YOU CAN BEAT LUNG CANCER:
Using Alternative/Integrative Interventions

Can you overcome lung cancer without harsh chemicals, surgery and debilitation? Are alternative interventions effective? Why do conventional physicians not use them? Can you prevent cancer recurrences and live into old age without chronic diseases and prescribed medications? This book answers these and other questions.

This is one of the most comprehensive books available on alternative treatments for lung cancer. It explains the treatments used successfully by a health professional/cancer survivor of 36 years and by some of the leading medical and health practitioners currently in the field. G. Edward Griffin, Author of World Without Cancer, The Politics of Cancer Therapy, and other books and films. Recipient of the Telly Award for Excellence in Television Production. President of American Media.

ABOUT THE AUTHOR: Dr Carl O Helvie (1932-) grew up in Gouverneur, New York and functioned as a nurse practitioner, educator, author, and researcher for 60 years. Most of his degrees and practice have been in public health and wellness. During his years in academia he wrote 10 books and book chapters, over 55 articles, gave 57 research papers around the United States and Europe, developed a nursing theory, and received funding for and established a nursing center and provided primary care for homeless and low income individuals and families. He also overcome lung cancer using natural interventions after being given 6 months to live by conventional medicine in 1974. Since retirement he has written two additional books and has been host of the holistic health radio show for the past 4 years. All of his current work since retirement from academia focuses on natural interventions for health problems. Applying these concepts in his own life he is now age 80 and free of chronic illnesses and prescribed medications dispite the average for a 75 year old of 3 chronic illnesses and 5 prescribed medications. In 1999 he received the Distinquised Career Award in Public Health from the American Publc Health Association, and most recently was listed in Wikipedia.

www.beatlungcancer.net

Steve Judd's Monthly Musings

A Modernistic Look at Pluto

Steve Judd

Pluto was discovered on February 18th, 1930, just over 88 years ago. Although its orbit is 248 years, it moves in an eccentric pattern, spending 30 years in Taurus, yet only 11 years in Scorpio and Sagittarius. Since it was first spotted, Pluto has completed fractionally over half an orbit and is now within one degree of opposition to the place it was at its discovery.

The mythological line of Pluto is clearly defined – Pluto in Greek myth is Hades, the first of five children of Cronos (Saturn), swallowed by their father lest they usurp him (as Cronos did with his father, Ouranus). Freed by his youngest brother Jupiter (Zeus), Pluto, Jupiter and the third brother, Neptune, divided the firmament between them, with Neptune taking the water world, Jupiter taking the overworld, and Pluto taking the underworld. Gradually, the ideas of Hades and Pluto became separate, with Hades eventually becoming Pluto's domain.

From an early date, Pluto's astrological values became clearly defined and have developed since that time. From a challenging perspective, Pluto has always been the planetary influence that deals with obsession and compulsion, intensity and extremes, as well as ideas of pain through crisis and trauma. At a neutral level, Pluto deals with purging, detoxing, cleansing, purification and elimination, whilst from a positive perspective, Pluto is transformation and regeneration, the caterpillar changing into the butterfly, the snake shedding its skin, and the phoenix rising from the ashes, reborn through crisis into a cleaner and clearer position.

Since the New Horizons space probe visit to Pluto in 2015, we've been able to gaze onto the face of Pluto, seeing for the first time that which has been hidden, or occluded, from us for nearly ninety years, suggesting that Pluto is beginning to give up its secrets. The first pictures from Pluto clearly show that half of the planetary surface is covered in white ice, whilst the rest is dark rock or carbon, emphasizing the Plutonic nature of black and white, yes and no, with little, if any, middle ground. The visit of the spacecraft also showed how the Plutonic system, with Pluto's attendant Moons of Charon, Nix, Kerberos, Hydra and Styx, is unique. Charon orbits Pluto twice for every one time that Pluto orbits Charon, creating a kind of binary system with an absolute void at the center – very fitting for Pluto's astrological meaning of depth, unconscious and subconscious, darkness at the center.

Recent discoveries of Pluto are pushing us to a new understanding of our own unconscious. With the advent of both personal and transpersonal psychology, individuals are being encouraged to go into their own personal dark and explore it, safe in the knowledge that there are no monsters in the caves of the unconscious, only dark. By going into these caves and bringing light into the dark and then returning and bringing dark into the light, we are creating a more unified and integrated sense of self. There cannot be light without also dark. They are equal and opposite.

As we become more aware of our own psychology, so we become more self-empowered to make decisions for ourselves that eliminate doubt. Merciless and mercenary are cruel and callous words, with no room for empathy or compassion, but ruthless is just yes or no, black or white with no middle ground. The position of Pluto in our individual birth charts is increasingly making us aware of our capacity for elimination and purging of self-doubt and the vacuous through being ruthless, whilst retaining the capacity for empathy and compassion – Pluto is beginning in certain astrological circles to be seen as the dark feminine as much as the dark masculine!

A strong Pluto in the birth chart basically means that you don't burn out; you keep going when everybody else falls by the wayside. You make and take the hard choices that others won't or can't. Pluto is setting you free and breaking your heart at the same time, to quote ABGT. It removes the capacity for doubt and elevates consciousness to a position of certainty, even if that certainty makes you realize things about yourself that aren't very nice. It takes you above and beyond the confines of normal emotional space and time, creating a world view that is absolute.

Many people make the mistake of identifying the astrological Pluto with the notion of being powerful, but that carries with it the idea of owning power, which in time will corrupt and twist the individual into the dark and negative side of Pluto, the manipulator and power broker.

Instead, the astrological Pluto is truly about being power filled, acting as a conduit and channel for Pluto's power and becoming an agent for transformation and a catalyst for change. Indeed, perhaps catalyst is a good word for Pluto – a catalyst doesn't heal or change others, they give others the power to heal or change themselves, making individuals more self-empowered and less dependent on others, which in turn helps transform the world.

As more and more people engage with Pluto and their own personal psychological states, so the doorways of the unconscious and subconscious become wider and more available to all. Perhaps as we get a foothold in the third millennium, so the emergence of Pluto into the light becomes more of a metaphor for an integrated transformation, both of ourselves and the planet we share.

In this light, a more shamanistic approach to life, the planet and our collective responsibility towards it is signified, and to quote Terence McKenna, "Not a moment too soon." Embrace Pluto. There is nothing to be scared of except fear itself. Pluto teaches us that death is not the end, merely the next step and that we are eternal, with physical death just being the jump from one dimension to another. We are all entitled to a good life and we are all entitled to a good death. Pluto, after all, is the planet of death and rebirth!

Steve Judd, late March 2018.

About the Author:

Steve Judd is a practicing astrologer with 40+ year's astrological experience. Check him out on YouTube or at www.stevejudd.com. []

The dream is specifically the utterance of the unconscious. just as the psyche has a diurnal side which we call consciousness, so also it has a nocturnal side: the unconscious psychic activity which we apprehend as dreamlike fantasy. - *Carl Jung*

Advertisements

Shamanic Healing
REGAIN YOUR SOVEREIGN SELF

The ancient art of shamanic healing can help you reconnect with your birthright ~ your gifts, talents, the right to manifesr your dreams, and more.

Cody Alexander is a highly trained and compassionate shamanic practitioner, skilled in guiding you to your true self, the person you came here to be.

For more information, or to schedule a long distance appointment, go to www.codyalexander.net, email healingpathways33@gmail.com, or call 719-458-9552.

Schedule your healing today!

Soul Balancing
There Is Always Hope

The actions of our past cannot be undone. However, the influence, emotions, triggers, and trauma of those actions can be!

Systems Buster - a process to lessen the intensity of negative chatter as well as the programs & systems that we've bought into.
Clearings - a process for the removal of entities & ET's as well as removing extreme trauma drama & patterns that keep playing out in your life.
Healings - a process that helps to heal & resolve where you are emotionally or mentally wounded or triggered.
Activations - a process that helps to turn on or activate your 5th Dimensional self so you can connect with who you really are.
Upgrades - a process that upgrades the programs & systems that we do want to keep running for our own well being.
Soul Retrievals - a process that helps to retrieve and bring back parts of yourself that have been lost or scattered.
PTSD (Trauma) - a process that returns you to a state of mind that allows you to more effectively move forward in your life.

Private & Couple Sessions • Harmonized Group Clearings • Intuitive Palm Readings • Home or Office Clearings • Object Clearings

Trixie Phelps
Soul Balancing Master Healer
720-340-1109
Trixie@SoulBalancing.World
www.SoulBalancing.World

Long-Distance Sessions Available
(Phone or Skype)

In-Person Sessions Available
(Longmont, CO)

Advertisements

The Winds of Change Association presents

The Unitive Life Audio Series

with Christina Donnell, Ph.D.
A nine-session audio series

For more information:
www.christinadonnell.com

"To awaken within the Absolute, and be its agent, is to be an energizing center in the times we live in."
~ CHRISTINA DONNELL

Optimizing Spinal Surgery

Dr. David Hanscom, M.D.

We live in an era of unprecedented knowledge and resources that were unimaginable just 50 years ago. It was only a little over 100 years ago that we even had anesthesia available to allow surgeons the time to perform their complex and often lengthy procedures. However, while technology has advanced, medicine has lost its focus on the most important aspect of healing – listening to the patient.

It's impossible to solve a problem in any arena without knowing the full extent of it. This is particularly true in the presence of an illness, in that the patient's environment may be stressful, which changes the body's chemical makeup. This creates an adverse environment that affects every organ in the body and results in multiple physical symptoms.

These environmental variables are well-documented in the medical literature and have been shown to negatively affect the outcomes of spinal surgery. Currently, the medical profession/culture is ignoring them, frequently resulting in catastrophic results:

• It is reported in over one thousand peer-reviewed research articles that anxiety, depression, catastrophizing, and fear avoidance, adversely affect the results of surgery.
o They are better predictors of outcome than the actual pathology.
• Shared decision-making regarding procedures with permanent sequelae is critical.
o A fusion for LBP (Lower Back Pain) is successful only about 25% of the time at two-year follow up.
• Surgeons cannot accurately assess patient stress in the office setting.
• Sleep is a well-documented factor that affects the perception of pain.
• Degenerative disc disease is a part of the normal aging process and has been shown to have little, if any, correlation with back pain.
• Any surgery performed in any part of the body can create chronic pain as an outcome of the procedure. It occurs 10-40% of the time and it can be permanent around 5-10% of time.
• High dose narcotics not only create a tolerance, but also increase the actual level of pain.
• Physical conditioning and activity are important in decreasing pain.
• Focused structured care can markedly improve both surgical and non-surgical outcomes.

Here is what is currently being done:
• Surgeons are monitored on productivity and discouraged from spending time with patients.
• Less than 10% of surgeons assess stress before making the decision to perform surgery. Therefore, there is little shared decision-making.
o Frequently, major life-altering decisions are made on the first visit with inadequate data and patient education.
• Surgeons feel they can assess mental stress in the clinic. Yet it's documented that they can do so less than 45% of the time.
• Sleep is rarely addressed by anyone.
• In spite of the overwhelming evidence that the outcomes of surgery for degenerative disc are poor and unpredictable, there are hundreds of thousands of them performed annually in the United States.
• Narcotic usage is seldom defined and stabilized before surgery.
• Although physical therapy is often prescribed, there is often no long term conditioning plan implemented.
• A multi-faceted approach to resolving chronic pain is often not available. Most physicians are not well trained to deal with chronic pain and dislike dealing with it.
• Surgery is simplistically viewed as the definitive solution. It is just one tool and is actually dangerous. Chronic pain is seldom mentioned as a complication of surgery.

About three years ago, I, along with my team, decided to become more systematic with our pre-surgical process. We coined the term, "prehab." We will not perform elective spine surgery unless the patient is willing to work through his or her part of the protocol for at least six weeks. I also no longer perform surgery for back pain.
• Surgical decisions are not made on the first visit.
*Specific educational material is available for a shared decision-making process on follow up visits.
• Psychosocial variables are obtained and acknowledged on the first visit.
o Anxiety/ anger/ depression assessed and treated.
o Must have some degree of improvement prior to proceeding with surgery.
• Sleep:
o Should be sleeping at least six hours per night, for more than six weeks.
• Medications defined and stabilized:
o Pain consultation if daily opiate intake > 100 mg of Morphine equivalent.

I have observed that patients' post-operative pain is less, rehab is easier, the outcomes are more consistently excellent, and there is a quicker return to full function. What has been surprising is that I have now seen dozens of patients who have had their pain resolve without surgery, in spite of having significant anatomical problems that I had planned on solving with surgery.

One woman presented to me with left leg pain, which she had been experiencing for over a year. Her MRI scan showed a pinched nerve that matched the pattern of pain. She seemed very straightforward, and the situation seemed so clear-cut that I decided to offer her an operation on her first visit. That's not my usual practice. I generally feel it's important for me to get to know my patients over several months before a decision involving a significant amount of risk is made.

As I walked out the door to get some educational materials about the proposed procedure, she said, "My daughter just died." I turned around and sat down. "My 32 year old daughter died a couple of months ago from cancer."

I told her that even before I knew much about chronic pain, I'd never perform surgery when someone was experiencing a severe personal stress or loss. I said that I wasn't willing to make a decision on this visit and to call me in a week.

In the meantime, I asked her to begin working on the tools on my website, www.backincontrol.com. She wasn't that happy with me, but she did call me back in a week and stated that she had decided to proceed with surgery. I told her I would sign her up and see her in a week for a pre-op appointment. She had begun the expressive writing exercises that are the foundation of the prehab process.

She came in with her husband on the next visit and asked me if she could delay the surgery for couple of weeks, because she was feeling a little better. When I saw her a month later for the final pre-operative visit, her pain was gone and never returned. She was now able to verbalize her loss to others and was more concerned about the effect of the loss on her husband.

Variations of this story occur in my clinic weekly. I have gone from dreading chronic pain, to being energized by people without hope regaining their lives – with or without surgery.

Chronic pain is a solvable problem. The first step is understanding it.

About the Author:

Dr. David Hanscom is a leading orthopedic spine surgeon at the Swedish Neuroscience Institute in Seattle, WA. Though he believes that surgery and medication have a role, he knows that these standard courses of treatment aren't what's needed to treat chronic pain. Instead, he provides the framework so the patient can find his or her solution, allowing them to live free of pain, forever. His method, which transforms all kinds of pain, including back, neck, arthritis, fibromyalgia, and migraines, is explained in BACK IN CONTROL: A Surgeon's Roadmap Out of Chronic Pain. []

Native American Quote:

"When you are in doubt, be still, and wait;

When doubt no longer exists for you then go forward with courage.

So long as mists envelop you, be still;

Be still until the sunlight pours through and dispels the mists

-As it surely will.

Then act with courage."

Ponca Chief White Eagle

Gran's Garden

Gran's Garden

Gwilda Wiyaka

Winter seemed to last forever! Thea couldn't wait for spring. In spring it got warm, the snow melted, and she and her brother, Tim, would get to visit Gran.

Visits with Gran were the best! Gran was wise and kind. She would show Thea how to fix delicious homemade goodies from things she had canned last fall. Gran had a beautiful backyard and a huge garden. But best of all, this year, in that garden was a special raised bed Gran had set aside, just for Thea and her brother Tim to plant their very own garden.

Gran had taught them you can't plant a garden in the snow and cold. It would kill the little seeds. They had to wait for spring.

When they visited Gran for spring break, she taught Thea and Tim how to start plants indoors by planting them in little pots. Gran called this "pushing." She explained that outdoors, the air and soil were still too cold to sprout seeds.

But the days had been getting longer. There was now enough light to support the seedlings if they were started indoors by a window. That way, they could get the light they needed and still be warm enough to grow. Gran told the children that every season had a purpose. Spring was the time for beginning things. If you worked with nature, you could "push" things a little to give them a head start. She explained that the seedlings would need to go outside at just the right time. If you started them too early – "pushed" them too hard – they would need to go outside before it was warm enough.

Gran had taken the children to a hardware store to purchase seeds and little pots. While they were there, they stopped to visit the baby chicks kept in big troughs under warm lights. It was time to begin growing chicks inside as well, Gran explained. They would have a head start by doing what she called "feathering out," so they could move outdoors sooner.

"Can we get some baby chicks to push, too?" Tim pleaded.

"Yeah, Gran, can we please?" Thea chimed in.

"Okay, but you will be responsible for cleaning their coop, feeding and watering them, and gathering eggs this summer while you are staying with me."

"Yeah!!" Tim and Thea yelled, jumping up and down in excitement.

Gran let them pick their chicks, and purchased a light to keep the chicks warm, a box for them to live in, and wood chips for bedding. They also needed a little feeder and watering dish, but Gran said she already had those at home.

They took the cute little chicks home and set everything up.

Thea decided then and there that spring was her favorite time of year!

The next time the children went to Gran's house, it was time to start working the soil in the raised bed Gran had set aside for them. Gran had a big pile of leaves and kitchen scraps in a wired off area that she called her "compost heap." Gran put some of the compost into a garden cart with some alpaca poo she got from the neighbor, stirred it all together and added worms that she called "garden hackles."

"Eeew," Thea complained, "That is just nasty, Gran!"

"Everything works together, Thea," Gran shared. "The fallen leaves, food scraps and poo from last year is the food for this year's garden. The worms put air and more fertilizer into the soil. We all work together. Everything depends upon everything else. It's the way life works."

All the seeds were different, with different needs. Gran showed the kids how to read the seed packets, to see which ones you started indoors, which ones you could put into the ground as soon as you could work the soil, and which ones you planted in the ground after danger of frost. She helped them plant each kind of seed at the proper depth and distance apart, cover them over, and mark the rows with little wooden popsicle sticks with the name of the plant on them.

"Now we need to water them and keep them moist so they can germinate," Gran informed.

"With the right amount of light, good, rich soil and water, the seeds will sprout and push up to get to the sun."

Thea and Tim couldn't wait until they started to grow. Every day during their visit, the children went out first thing in the morning to look, but nothing had changed.

"Nothing is happening," Thea complained.

"Oh, there is plenty happening, Thea. Don't you remember when Tim was growing in your mommy's tummy?"

"Yeah."

"At first you couldn't see anything, right?"

"Yeah, but then she got a baby bump!" Thea exclaimed.

"Just keep watching. Water and care for your garden, even though it doesn't look like anything is going on. Everything starts in the invisible," Gran advised.

The children faithfully watered their little pots and the outside garden. Finally one day, the earth formed little bulges.

"It's a baby bump, the garden has baby bumps, Gran!" Thea and Tim shouted excitedly one morning. "It's magic!"

"Yes, little ones, life is magic," Gran agreed.

To be continued in the next edition of The New Age Chronicles.[]

Hopi Prayer to The Great Spirit

Let me walk in beauty, and make my eyes ever behold the red and purple sunset. Make my hands respect the things you have made and my ears sharp to hear your voice. Make me wise so that I may understand the things you have taught my people. Let me learn the lessons you have hidden in every leaf and rock.

I seek strength, not to be greater than my brother, but to fight my greatest enemy, Myself.

Make me always ready to come to you with clean hands and straight eyes.

Asquali, Kawquai

A Voice Saved My Life

Bill Bennett

I was in New Orleans, driving to the airport to get the first flight back to LA. It was dark, before dawn, and as I approached an intersection, I heard a voice. It said, "Slow down." I thought I'd imagined it. It was so weird. I'd never heard anything like this before. I still hadn't fully woken up. Maybe it was a dream. So I ignored it.

I went to speed up, to make sure I got through on the green light. I was worried about missing my flight. As I went to accelerate, the voice said again, "Slow down." It was more emphatic this time. So I slowed down.

As I entered the intersection, a huge truck ran a red light on a cross street. It hurtled through the intersection, missing me by inches. If I hadn't listened to that voice and followed its advice, I would have been killed. I pulled up on the other side of the intersection, shaking with adrenalin, and three questions hit me hard:

- What was that voice?
- Where did it come from?
- Why did it save my life?

I'm a filmmaker, so I set about trying to answer those questions by making a film about it. Some eighteen years later – yes, eighteen years later! – that film is now in release. It's called, PGS – Intuition is your Personal Guidance System.

Why did it take so long to make the film? Because first I had to figure out what intuition actually is, and how it works. You might think that's easy, but in fact, I found it to be a very complex and personally challenging endeavor, to bring something as intangible and ephemeral as intuition into an easy to understand and accessible form, without dumbing it down, and without in any way diminishing the sacredness of what it truly is.

To do that, I had to become intuitive myself – and that's what took the longest time. Because to become intuitive, I had to go on a spiritual journey. And that's not what I wanted to do at the start. I knew it would involve change, and when it came down to it, I didn't want to change. I was quite happy living my ego-based, small-self life, thank you very much!

But change I did – the film forced me to change! – and now I live a fully intuitive life.

What does that mean? I live a fully intuitive life?

Well, it means that I acknowledge guidance, I accept that guidance exists to keep me on my destiny path through life, and I allow myself to work with guidance each moment of each day.

What is guidance? When you pare it all down to the essentials, guidance is actually a divine messaging service. Intuition is a way that Source, or the Creator, or the Universe, or God – whatever term you wish to use – connects with you to help you make the right choices in life.

We are all defined by our choices, and mostly we make choices based on fear, whether we fully acknowledge that or not. Fear manifests in ways such as making a choice based on what's accepted, or what our friends or family think is the right choice to make, or what so-called common sense would have us do, or what we believe will deliver us the best outcome in the long run.

These choices, decisions, are dictated by fear, which comes from rational thinking. Our ego. Our intellect. They might be at variance to what our heart wants us to do, or what we simply know is the right thing to do. That sense of knowing, that heart-sense, is our intuition – our personal guidance system – telling us to ignore our ego, ignore our intellect, and go with our gut, go with our heart, go with that innate sense of knowing what's the right thing to do.

What I've discovered is that we all have intuition. We're born with it. It's a system that's as legitimate as our circulatory system, our immune system, and our other flesh-and-bones physiological systems. It's just that our intuition is a system that exists in our energetic realm. That's why western science has such a hard time coming to terms with intuition – because they don't yet have the instruments to measure it, and determine how it works.

But we know it works because we experience intuitive hits every day – whether it's as simple and basic as an intuitive impulse to trust someone you might work with, or to like someone you meet at a cafe.

How do you begin to access your latent intuitive powers? I outline five steps in my movie:

- STOP
- LISTEN
- ASK
- TRUST
- FOLLOW

To begin, you first have to stop, to allow yourself to hear your intuitive voice, or to sense your intuitive impulses that might come to you through your gut, your heart, your sense of knowing – even through coincidence or synchronicity. If you're constantly being distracted by the busyness of life around you, it becomes much more difficult to pay attention to the efforts your Personal Guidance System is taking to connect with you.

Once you stop, you can listen.

At times, you have to ask for guidance. And it will come, if the request is sincere. You can ask in meditation, you can ask in prayer, but you can also ask in a moment of stillness. Walking along the beach, or sitting on a bench in a park, can provide you with the calm you might require to ask in a connected and pure way.

Trust is the biggie – to trust the Universe, you first have to trust yourself, and to trust yourself you have to clean up your act. Get rid of anger, get rid of envy, jealousy, competitiveness, fear of loss, fear in all its various manifestations – all these things that contaminate your energy fields. How do you do that, you might ask, living in the real world?

Well, I can't answer for you – I can only tell you what I did. I got to a point of realization that I am an aspect of the Divine, same as everyone else. And as soon as I realized that, everything else dropped away. Nothing was important anymore, other than that realization. I dropped off all those lower-energy frequencies which, for so long, had kept me mired in anger, fear, competitiveness, jealousy – the list was sad and long.

And having released all that stuff – that ugly stuff – I was then able to trust. Because I trusted myself. All the issues I'd had with self-esteem were no longer an issue. I was free at last to trust.

It's one thing to trust: you then have to follow through with guidance. We can, on one level, get to the point of trusting our intuition, but if we don't act on it, then the whole thing is a complete waste of time. Putting into action what our guidance directs us to do can be terrifying, but we have to do it, because we have to trust that our Personal Guidance System – our intuition – has an overview we can't ever see or even understand. But it's leading us ultimately to the full expression of who we really are.

Meet the Author:

One of Australia's most respected filmmakers, Bill Bennett has 40+ Aussie Oscar nominations for his movies and numerous Australian and international awards, including Australia's Oscar for Best Picture and Best Director, and Australia's Emmy twice for Most Outstanding Documentary (television). His films have been distributed through several Hollywood studios, screened at some of the world's most prestigious film festivals, at the New York Museum of Modern Art, and in Official Selection at the Cannes Film Festival.

An Adjunct Professor of Creative Industries at one of Australia's largest universities, his first novel (in a Young Adult trilogy) – Palace of Fires – has just been published by Penguin Random House. []

POSITIVE QUOTES:

Love yourself. It is important to stay positive because beauty comes from the inside out. - *Jenn Proske*

Keep your face to the sunshine and you cannot see a shadow. - *Helen Keller*

Once you replace negative thoughts with positive ones, you'll start having positive results. - *Willie Nelson*

Work hard, stay positive, and get up early. It's the best part of the day.
- *George Allen, Sr.*

In every day, there are 1,440 minutes. That means we have 1,440 daily opportunities to make a positive impact. - *Les Brown*

In order to carry a positive action we must develop here a positive vision. - *Dalai Lama*

The difference between a dream and reality, is doing it. - *Rob McConnell*

Optimizing Your Intuitive Skills

3 Points for Optimizing Your Intuitive Skills

Diane Brandon

Intuition is a wonderful tool to use in our lives, and increasing numbers of people are discovering its benefits for themselves. That said, as someone who has both utilized intuition and taught intuitive skills to others for many years, I know that there are ins and outs to intuition that may not always make using it smooth sailing. The good news is that these are not insurmountable obstacles, and we can optimize our intuitive skills by being mindful of some of these ins and outs.

The following points should allow you to use your intuition more adeptly in your life and reap more of it its rewards.

Point # 1: Intuition is Not a One-Size-Fits-All Faculty

Have you found yourself looking to others who are skilled with their intuition as examples to follow? Have you felt that you needed to conform to others' examples, and thought that you came up short with your intuition?

When I first started using my intuition professionally, I felt that I didn't know what I was doing. I kept feeling that my intuition should be direct and unmistakable and that I needed to see things visually. In other words, I assumed this was how intuition worked for those who were skilled with it, and that it couldn't work in any other way.

This is not at all true! Intuition is highly individual. It is far from a one-size-fits-all skill. Just because you may admire someone whose intuition speaks to him or her in visual images does not mean that this is how your intuition will work for you.

It's very important to learn how your intuition speaks to you, not how it speaks to others. Do you visually see things? Do you feel or sense things? Do you have an inner voice that speaks to you? There are many, many ways in which we can be spoken to, and intuitive information can come to us in many different ways and forms.

I would start off with befriending your intuition as it is. Let it appear to you and speak to you in its own way, while you allow yourself to recognize just how it's doing this. It's very important to start off with your own experience with it, knowing that how you're spoken to is perfectly fine. How we're spoken to is how we're supposed to be spoken to.

Over time, you may find your intuition begins to speak to you in additional ways, especially if you are open to it doing so. This is what happened to me.

So start off with your own particular ways and forms, and then be open to more over time.

Point # 2: Intuition is Not Foolproof

We may expect once we are using our intuition that the intuitive information we get will always be reliable and correct. Unfortunately, this is not true. Intuition is far from foolproof.

First of all, I'm a firm believer that we get the information we're supposed to have. If we could "game the system" and always get correct information, there would be less likelihood of our unfolding and growing. And unfolding and growing is one of the major reasons why we're here on this planet in a human form. We may get information that's not correct, which then leads us to have experiences from which we learn and strengthen.

Secondly, our personal stuff (wants, fears, needs, biases, mindsets, etc.) will often creep in and contaminate the intuitive information we get, rendering it much less reliable. This is part of being a human and having a human psyche, and it can make using our intuition more of a challenge and less reliable.

It's very important to be mindful of this "loosey-goosey" aspect of intuition, making it more like jello that we can't rely on, rather than a firm structure.

Being aware of our personal stuff, while trying to clear it or at least minimize it, can help, as can some methods of receiving intuitive information. (See the next point.) That said, it's quite helpful to be aware of this aspect of intuition.

Point # 3: We Don't Have to Wait for Intuitive Information to Come to Us Spontaneously

Most people experience their intuition when information comes to them spontaneously. As a result, many people may tend to feel they have to wait for their intuition to speak to them – when it feels like it, so to speak.

One wonderful aspect of intuition is that we don't need to wait for it to appear. Instead, we can invite it in and can even learn how to access it on demand. I have been doing this for over 25 years, and numerous intuitives do it.

I refer to the method I use as "tuning in." It involves shifting my level of consciousness, blanking my mind out, posing a question, and waiting for information, in any form it may come. (I detail this method at length in my book, Intuition for Beginners: Easy Ways to Awaken Your Natural Abilities.) This method not only allows us to access intuitive information on demand, but also can allow us to receive information that is clearer and more reliable. In being clear in using this method, we are more apt to bypass our personal stuff, so that it doesn't affect or contaminate the information we receive.

Learning to tune in to receive information can allow you to optimize and grow your intuitive skills, while also maximizing the reliability of the information you get.

So take note of these points, and watch your intuition growing in a beautiful way.

About the Author:

Diane Brandon is an Integrative Intuitive Counselor, teacher, former radio host, and coach, as well as the author of Born Aware: Stories & Insights from Those Spiritually Aware Since Birth, Intuition for Beginners: Easy Ways to Awaken Your Natural Abilities, Dream Interpretation for Beginners: Understand the Wisdom of Your Sleeping Mind, and Invisible Blueprints. Born and raised in New Orleans, she has an A.B. from Duke University and did Master's work at University of North Carolina. Her website is www.dianebrandon.com.[]

Intuition and Premonitions

Dawson Church

On Oct 9, 2017, my home and office in California were incinerated by a massive wildfire. My wife, Christine, and I got out with moments to spare.

We woke up at 12:45 a.m. and saw the flames racing toward us. Running to the car, we got out just ahead of the inferno. Many of our neighbors weren't so lucky. Reports from fire fighters later estimated that the fire traveled the length of a football field every three seconds.

Forty-two people didn't escape in time. But thousands did. Why?

In the weeks since the fire, that time of 12:45 a.m. keeps cropping up in conversations with friends and neighbors. Many of them report waking up at that exact time. When asked why they woke up, they can't explain it. After they awoke, they might have smelled smoke or seen the glow of the fire on the horizon. But what woke them up in the first place?

Many people seem to have premonitions just before disasters. The New York City police department produced the first official estimate of the death toll from the attacks on September 11, 2001 – 6,659 dead. It was based on reasonable estimates of the number of people who should have been at their desks in the Twin Towers on a weekday morning.

But the final death toll was only 2,753. Where were the missing people? Many were evacuated successfully, but many others reported unusual circumstances that kept them away. Some had premonitions of disaster. Others had disturbing dreams that led them to alter their routines. These subtle signals may be a relic of the sixth sense that human beings have had since the dawn of history.

A remote chain of 500 islands called the Andamans and Nicobars lies off the Bay of Bengal. Andaman Island itself is inhabited by an aboriginal tribe of hunter-gatherers called the Jarawa. They are fiercely independent and self-sufficient, rejecting all contact with outsiders (National Geographic, 2005).

On December 26, 2004, a massive tsunami struck the coast, with the Andamans and Nicobars directly in its path. Anthropologists feared that all 250 members of the Jarawa tribe had been washed away. On the neighboring island of Nicobar, 1,458 people died.

However, when government helicopters arrived to render aid, the Jarawa fired arrows at them. Eventually, seven men emerged from the forest wearing loincloths and amulets. They told aid workers that not a single member of the tribe had died (Lagorio, 2005). Just before the tsunami struck, the entire tribe had moved deep into the jungle.

In my book Mind to Matter: The Astonishing Science Behind How Your Brain Creates Material Reality, I summarize over 400 studies (Church, 2018). They show a link between the electromagnetic fields of individual human beings, and planetary information fields. The Earth's North and South poles remind us that we live on a giant magnet, and many animals are able to sense these geomagnetic fields. Dolphins, cows, and migrating birds are all able to perceive them.

The human brain also contains strings of magnetic particles. These may be sensitive to the Earth's field, picking up information as well. Rollin McCraty, director of research at HeartMath institute, says, "We're all like little cells in the bigger Earth brain – sharing information at a subtle, unseen level that exists between all living systems, not just humans, but animals, trees, and so on." (McCraty, 2015)

Human beings are part of the web of life. Modern humans are capable of picking up on the subtle signals inherent in nature, just as the Andaman islanders did. I also believe that, with practice, we can hone our abilities to tune in to global natural cycles. Like any skill, the more it is practiced, the stronger it becomes. Meditation, prayer and spiritual practice can all put us back in tune with natural cycles larger than our individual lives. 12:45 am is my personal daily reminder of the presence of these global rhythms.

About the Author:

Dawson Church is the author of Mind to Matter: The Astonishing Science of How Your Brain Creates Material Reality. He has conducted many scientific studies of health and epigenetics. He shares scientific breakthroughs on gene expression and peak performance at DawsonGift.com.
His website: https://dawsonchurch.com/
Links: https://dawsonchurch.com/links/

References:

- Church, D. (2018). Mind to matter: The astonishing science of how your brain creates material reality. Carlsbad, CA: Hay House.
- Lagorio, C. (2005, January 4). Ancient tribe survives tsunami. CBS News. Retrieved November 24, 2017, from www.cbsnews.com/news/ancient-tribe-survives-tsunami
- McCraty, R. (2015). Could the energy of our hearts change the world? Retrieved November 24, 2017, from www.goop.com/wellness/spirituality/could-the-energy-of-our-hearts-change-the-world
- National Geographic. (2005, January 24). Did island tribes use ancient lore to evade tsunami? National Geographic News. Retrieved November 24, 2017, from news.nationalgeographic.com/news/2005/01/0125_050125_tsunami_island.html

MISSION: EVOLUTION with Gwilda Wiyaka

Past Episodes Include:

- **Kathleen O'Keef-Kanavos** - Hidden Precognitive and Diagnostic Power of Dreams
- **Stephanie Mines** - The Shock Factor: Evolutionary Challenges of our Time
- **Patricia Albere** - Mutual Awakening
- **Bryan Robinson, PhD** - Balance, Resilience and Evolution
- **Marcelle Pick** - Fine Tuning the Evolving Body
- **Craig S Webb** - Lucid Living
- **Michelle Fondin** - Chakras as Evolutionary Gateways
- **Mitchell Nicholas Gerber** - Into the Shadow - Organ Harvesting and Genocide
- **Nancy Hyvarinen** - Removing the Blocks to Personal Evolution
- **Robert Kopecky** - Near-Death Experience
- **Robert Levine**: The Boundless Self
- **Meriflor Toneatto** - Difference Makers
- **Corinne Zupko** - The Trauma Trap

You can listen to all of the interesting interviews simply by going to....

www.missionevolution.org

A 'X' Zone Broadcast Network Production

Soul Retrieval and EMDR

Soul Retrieval and EMDR: Integrating Shamanism and Psychotherapy

Edie Stone, MA, LPC,
Certified Shamanic Journey Guide

The Lost Inner Child

The Little Girl was scared and confused. Her uncle was driving so fast that the curves in the road were making her tummy sick. Her Mommy was very quiet, so she stayed still and didn't talk either. She didn't cry, she was trying to be brave for Mommy.

Then they were at a hospital. Her uncle was yelling at a nurse to let her into the room to see her Daddy. He was afraid her Daddy would die without seeing his Little Girl again. She was afraid of how loud her uncle was.

Her Daddy was in a bed. He had tubes in his nose. He had tubes on his arms. His voice was very weak. He told her he loved her.

40 years later, she is crying in my office. She is not sure why.

She had come in because she was anxious and had started having panic attacks. Her kids were growing up. She wasn't sure what career path to take. She seemed spaced out, not very present. Her breathing was shallow.

She didn't mention her father's heart attack; she didn't see the connection yet.

If I were just a clinical counselor, if I just looked at her symptoms, I would give her a diagnosis of Generalized Anxiety Disorder, noting the panic symptoms. We'd work with relaxation skills, reframe negative self-talk, develop a plan including exercise and career counseling. These are all good interventions, and she would feel better. For a while.

But that would be missing the deeper picture.

As a holistic psychotherapist, I am interested in the whole story. Later, when I heard about her father's heart attack, I started to realize this wasn't just a mid-life career crisis, but that she had suffered unresolved emotional trauma. It wasn't violent trauma, and it wasn't emotional abuse. She wasn't volatile or highly reactive – except for the new panic symptoms, she wasn't stuck in fight/flight responses.

But she seemed disconnected, not aware of her body. Her breathing was shallow. That is an important cue. As I got to know her better, I explained the "freeze response."

The Freeze Response, Trauma, and the Lost Inner Child

Freeze is a recent addition to "fight/flight," which is the arousal of the autonomic nervous system that we learned about in high school biology.

The freeze response happens when an animal or human is threatened with danger, but can neither fight back nor run away. Rabbits freeze. A deer caught in the headlights is a classic freeze response.

Often, children can't fight back or run away from painful or dangerous situations. Sometimes they freeze. Sometimes they cut themselves off from their feelings. Sometimes they dissociate, or "space out," or go numb. Sometimes the numbness turns into depression. Later, as teens, sometimes they cut themselves to release their feelings, or restrict eating to distance themselves even more from their bodies.

I have studied trauma theory, EMDR – an excellent trauma treatment, Gestalt and family systems, and learned how all of us have self-parts — sub-personalities such as an Inner Critic or Judge, an Inner Teen or Rebel, a Worker Bee, a Lazy Bum, a Victim, a Rescuer, a whole cast of characters.

We all have an Inner Child. Actually, we have a number of Inner Children of various ages and stages. If we suffered in childhood, our Inner Children may still be holding onto the pain, the wounds, the rage, or the freeze in various ways. If an Inner Child was hurt enough or frozen too often, it may have hidden, split off, or seemingly disappeared. The Adult Part may not realize the Inner Child is still split off, still suffering.

The freeze response often accompanies trauma and can contribute to symptoms of PTSD. Freeze can also contribute to a spiritual illness known as Soul Loss.

Shamanic Journeys and Soul Retrieval

Shamanism is an ancient practice that treats spiritual illness. As a Certified Shamanic Journey Guide, I help clients ease into a naturally altered state of consciousness called a shamanic journey.

Some shamanic journeys are exploratory, with the intention of meeting and forming an ongoing relationship with Spirit Guides of all kinds … Power Animals, Teachers, Healers, Ancestors, Saints, Angels, Light Beings, Gods/Goddesses, Source.

Power Recoveries are journeys focused on regaining power or energy that was lost, taken, or given away at various times in the client's life. This can be an important stage in working with trauma.

Some journeys are focused specifically on Soul Retrieval.

Soul Retrieval is usually done with the shamanic practitioner journeying on behalf of their client. The practitioner may visit a "Cave of Souls" or other metaphorical location where a Soul Part may be "stuck," return with it, then return it to the client.

I don't journey on behalf of clients, as some shamanic practitioners do. Because I am a therapist, I support and gently guide clients as they take their own deep journey to reconnect with their own Lost Inner Child or Fractured Soul Part of any age. I have found that this process leads to profound emotional experiences and deeper integration.

EMDR and Soul-Retrieval for Integrative Healing

Clients need to be ready for Soul Retrieval, and also willing to spend time tending to the Soul Part that they bring back. They should want to really get to know and nourish that part of them that was lost, hidden, or fragmented.

But if their Soul Loss was from childhood, an abusive relationship, war trauma, or other intense events, clients often need support in learning skills for emotional containment and positive self-care.

EMDR is a type of therapy that helps them learn those skills in safe, incremental steps, and to experience remembering painful events in safe, controlled ways.

EMDR has been developed to treat trauma, but it is also effective for grief, anxiety, fear of public speaking, stuck relationship patterns, and other issues.

Trauma and fear-based memories are stored in the mid-brain, especially the right amygdala. (You can visualize the brain by folding your fingers around your thumb. The thumb is the mid-brain, the two middle fingers are the frontal lobes, pointer and pinky are the temporal lobes. The two parts of the amygdala are near the center.)

The amygdala takes information coming in from the senses, and makes an instant decision to instruct the body and brain to go on alert if there is a threat. The amygdala can save your life, but it is not good at turning itself off if the threat is intense or ongoing.

Unprocessed memories in the amygdala can lead to volatile behaviors, physical reactivity, chronic medical conditions, and/or freeze patterns such as numbness or dissociation. There also can be a sense that there is something missing in life, depression, or alienation from parts of the self. These are also symptoms of Soul Loss or Soul Fragmentation.
Rhythms of Healing

EMDR uses simple bi-lateral rhythms – eye movements, left/right tones, or alternating vibrations (like holding two flip-phones) – to help process traumatic or painful memories.
Researchers have found that the alternating rhythms of EMDR help relieve highly charged emotional memories in several ways, including finally getting neurons in the amygdala to discharge. The great thing about this process is that the client does not have to understand any of this information about the brain. It just happens in the brain when the client is ready and the conditions are right.

Many shamans also use rhythm to heighten and synchronize experiences in journeys and ceremonies, including drumbeats, rattles, ankle bells, singing bowls, mouth harps, and dance.

(Continued on Page 26)

**For The Very Best Of
Paranormal / Parapsychology
New Age Radio Programming 24/7/365
There Is Only One Radio Network
That Supplys The World...
www.XZBN.net**

Soul Retrieval and EMDR: Integrating Shamanism and Psychotherapy

Continued from Page 25

Brain Waves and Dream Waves

The felt experience of journeying is like a long lucid dream.

Shamanic journeys, supported by a driving rhythm, induce a vivid altered state of consciousness, often with intense images. Like a lucid dream, it is a state in which clients need to allow the imagery to arise naturally, yet can still exert some direction of will.

The experience of EMDR is like a set of short lucid dreams.

Research indicates that EMDR produces brain waves similar to those in Slow Wave Sleep, but stronger.* Experiences can be intense, emotionally and/or visually. Clients need to allow the process to flow, while maintaining some direction. There is a strange dual awareness: being vividly in the painful past, while feeling safe in the office.

Clients allow themselves to touch into the pain of an Inner Child, or a Lonely Teen, or a Wounded Warrior for a short time. They let themselves feel a little bit, then they come back. As clients allow feelings to arise for a short time with the alternating rhythm, gradually, amazingly, the pain drains away.

Images with no words now have a narrative. Memories that would erupt into the present now are placed in the past. Finally it is clear: that was then, this is now.

Soul Retrieval - Where Science and Shamanism Meet

Things got interesting for the client with the Frozen Inner Child when she realized that her father was 54 when he almost died. He lived for several years, but he was weak and struggled to breathe.

She was now 54. Her breath was shallow, and she was having panic attacks.
There was a mysterious quality about this that led me to integrate aspects of Soul Retrieval and EMDR therapy.

Preparation for EMDR usually starts with helping the client visualize a "safe space" that they can start from and return to. Clients who are already kind of spaced out usually love to journey out of the body. So in this case, I encouraged her to do the opposite, to focus on her physical sensations and emotions.

I also gave her shamanic homework: to spend time in nature between sessions, and to sit next to a tree and feel herself growing roots.
I led her through a couple of short journeys, using the alternating rhythms, to connect with her Spirit Guides, including protective and nurturing figures.

With Soul Retrieval, the goal is to bring the soul back fairly quickly, then work with integration. If this had been a case of child abuse, I would have taken that direction. But this was a case of numbness, and loss of voice and energy.

With EMDR, the protocol is to help clients to stay with their feelings and sensations, in tolerable amounts for a short set. They bring their awareness back to the room briefly, then repeat with the next set. When the client did this, the Frozen Child finally started to cry. She couldn't remember if she cried when she saw her Daddy, but she was crying now.

As I encouraged her to sob, her chest expanded and her hands started to shake. She moved her hands to her chest, so I encouraged her to tap there. She felt her heart breaking and finally coming alive again. Tingling and rushes of energy pulsed through her feet and legs. (For a trauma therapist, these are all good signs of release.)

Then the Spirit Realm took over.
Her father appeared to her.
He told her how much he loved her. He said he was proud of how hard she had studied. He thanked her for helping her mother, they were together now and happy again. And he even gave her some career advice.

Today, she feels more in touch with her body. She has realized how often she holds her breath, and works with a soft outbreath to continue releasing her old freeze pattern, and to come back into the present moment. She sees how much of an impact her experience at 10 years old has affected her career, and is reaching for bigger options. And she is able to be more tender and playful with her Inner Child.

About the Author:

Edie Stone, MA, LPC, is a Holistic Psychotherapist and Soul-Centered Counselor in Boulder, CO. She has been a Certified Shamanic Journey Guide since 1995. She loves helping people reclaim their power, integrity, creativity, and joy. She also teaches shamanism and dreamwork.

Edie's Website: www.ediestone.com and www.shamanicjourneys.net.

THE XZBN IS ALWAYS LOOKING FOR RADIO SHOWS AND HOST FOR OUR RADIO BROADCAST NETWORKS!

If you think that you have what we are looking for in a radio show / host, email programming@xzbn.net and a member of our programming staff will contact you.

www.xzbn.net

Dreamtime and Shamanism

The Dreamtime and Shamanism

Sandra Corcoran, M.Ed.

The word shamanism relates to the beliefs and practices of a shaman.

What is a shaman? One definition is, "a man or woman capable of reaching altered states of consciousness in order to interact with the world of spirit and transcendent energies." They do that in order to manifest something, be that a healing or a given message, into this waking reality for an individual or their community.

The term shaman initially derived from the Tungusic language of the peoples of eastern Siberia. However, the essence of the word has entered the popular lexicon to encompass indigenous tribal peoples of all lands—First Nations, Aboriginal, East Indian, the Far East, South and Central America—as healers, practitioners, those that prophesize and those that dream while working with the world of living energy.

What is the dreamtime? The dreamtime was initially a concept used to describe the Australian Aboriginal People's belief that the pattern of creation was laid down by the ancestors, way back in the beginning of time, the Dreamtime. As such, all worldly knowledge is acquired through the ancestors, informing both the land and the soul. Today, the dreamtime has also acquired its own expanded definition as "the landscape of an individual's nocturnal dream content."

No one has to be a shaman, medicine person, or healer to become a dreamer. Dreaming is a gift we are all born with. Often in my work, I hear people say, "But I never dream." Everyone dreams. You might not remember your dreams, or have yet uncovered a method to access your nocturnal wisdom, but you do dream.

Neither do we need crystals or subliminal hemi-sync recordings. We do not need to become a dream nagual or specialize in Buddhist yoga dream practices. We do not need to do special rituals or go to sacred sites. Although any of those tools, models, or concepts may well expand one's potential to become more conscious or lucid within the dream state, the ability to dream exists in everyone, from the time we were in utero, possibly even before life began, and will continue through life, to our death and what lays beyond.

My Native mentors referred to the dreamtime as the "little death," because the dream provides a container for us to retrieve messages as we learn how to consciously cross from sleeping to waking, and also to inform us as we traverse this lifetime and move towards death. This means the dream content can prepare for that which needs to end, be that one's life, or some aspect of life that no longer serves our waking state. As one of my Native teachers said, "As your dreams teach you to become conscious of what needs to change in your life, you can't walk stupid on the Earth anymore." Understanding the dream's message thus supports our personal evolution.

Dreams offer an opportunity to tap the unconscious Self and reveal to the waking self, vital information through symbolism, universal archetypes, the dream's mood, and the dream's characters. In my dream training with my indigenous elders, one of the most important aspects of a dream is "its feeling." The curiosity and clarity provoked by the dream "story" can untangle feelings we may not have brought to consciousness in the day-to-day activities that distract us. Discovery of the Self is one of the many things that motivates the dreamer. Shamans, Medicine People, Buddhist lucid dream practitioners all know this; it is why they use the dreamtime to interpret many of life's seeming vagaries.

Where a word elicits a meaning, a symbol contains an entire concept. The brilliant psychotherapist, Carl Jung, incorporated the collective archetypes as part of his dream theory. He suggested that within the dream, emotions translate into images, and those images expose what lay hidden deep within the individual. In this regard, understanding the symbology of one's dream and using that information to help raise one's consciousness, supports that consciousness and dreaming go hand-in-hand. Our dreams are an extraordinary gift, in that they offer direct communication between the individual and the divine planes of being; they do not require any intermediary. In that sense, we are each our own shaman, culling information to support knowing ourselves better. The dreamtime extends beyond time, space, dimensionality, and breath, informing the "I" that exists within the "I AM." Shamans teach that the human spirit is always in contact with the higher spiritual realms, even if one has no awareness of this unity in their ordinary state of consciousness. Although dreaming isn't the only pathway to open those portals, it is ours, it is constant, it is readily available, and it is affordable.

My long-time dream mentor, the late Grandmother Twylah Hurd Nitsch of the Seneca People (part of the Iroquois Confederacy or Five Nations Peace League), taught me how to decode dreams, as part of my personal "medicine" skills and for later use in my therapeutic practice. Dream decoders usually come to this training through a personal calling, and are taught how to traverse the dream world to heal and inform. Gram suggested that culture reflects the measure of our self-discipline, and as such, our consciousness. She said the discipline one takes to understand and decode their dreams, both honors our capacity as sovereign beings and expands our consciousness. During one of her many lessons on the variety, quality and function of dreams, she once told me that, "The Creator has offered the gift of the dreamtime to every creature; it is a gift of peace." Gram said when the world understands peace as one people, we will have created a new dream.

There have been volumes written on dreams from psychological, mythological, indigenous and/or cultural perspectives. I was taught that dreams help us hold onto our vital energy, even though they are super sensory and don't always make sense at first glance. Like learning a foreign language or understanding a lover, we need to practice, listen, observe, and pay attention to their content and disposition in order to be able to uncover their import and wisdom. Whether one's dreams are short or epic, they are sacred tools that have the capacity to move us toward self-discovery.

Dreams show us that we are not limited to one way of being, doing, experiencing or choosing. The very fabric of the dream offers the understanding that we exist everywhere and are not separated from the Source of all Life. All my shamanic mentors have stressed the importance of understanding that fact, and the responsibility that comes with it. As Gram Twylah suggested, "The dreamtime offers an expanded 'seeing and being,' making dreams the universe's gift of Remembrance."

About the Author:

Sandra Corcoran, M.Ed., is an integrative coach, shamanic teacher, writer, indigenously trained dream decoder, and Thoth Tarot reader. Author of Shamanic Awakening and the meditative CD, Souled Out, she co-created the STAR Process™; a spirit retrieval modality in '91. Mentored by indigenous wisdom-keepers for over 35 years, she has taught throughout North, South and Central America, England, Ireland, Italy and Egypt. A contactee, she worked with the late Dr. John Mack and Roberta Colasanti of PEER, studied through the Academy of Future Sciences, and offers workshops, readings, and yearly sacred journeys nationally and internationally. Website: www.starwalkervisions.com

Caves of Power

Caves of Power (The Hidden Power Inside All of Us)

Sergio Magaña

For ancient Mexicans, the concept of what is traditionally known as a cave was something very interesting to explore, since it entails different and various meanings.

First of all, a cave refers to all of that which is hidden inside of us, as well as to what is hidden within mother earth. If we give this idea a modern meaning, we will see that it is an immediate reference to what we now identify as the unconscious, which consists of several layers:

the part of you that's currently creating or reflecting yourself; the idea you have about yourself; the story that's an energy inside your mind; the internal voice derived from the knowledge of that which we believe to be true, and that often makes us limit ourselves with thoughts such as, "This is incurable," "I'm not good enough"; what we really feel and don't want to face; our sexual desires; the part of us known to the ancient ones as "the enemy," which is none other than the self-destructive force that resides in all of us; the part of us that instinctively picks fights; the internal part that makes us give in to our weaknesses over and over again, just like the false ego that keeps us under the illusion that we are superior or inferior to those around us.

On the other hand, the cave also contains:

the part of us which is capable of overcoming all of our weaknesses; the possibility of gaining access to a perception in which we are able to see the truth; that there are no differences between what we consider to be beautiful and what we consider to be ugly, young or old, life or death, which would in turn enable us to control this dream that we call life, as well as make it possible for us to use the power of our own cave or interior to help the collective.

All of these teachings are present in the ancient knowledge of those who were known as the Black Tezcatlipoca, the smoking mirror, the force behind everything we know.

In a second line of thought, scholars talk about a pilgrimage of the ancient Aztecs that lasted 260 days, from a city that many consider mythical and others real. It was named Aztlan, described as a place of white houses, lots of herons, and where people were good, evolved and spoke Nahuatl (the language used by Aztecs, Toltecs and many other indigenous groups currently). The pilgrimage would go on until they reached a certain spot where they would find a symbol consisting of an eagle, standing on top of a cactus, devouring a snake. This sign was supposedly found on a small island located in present-day Mexico City.

According to oral tradition, during the pilgrimage, these groups lived for a time inside caves known as Chicomoztoc (the cave of power). Many consider these caves to be a mythical place, while others are convinced that they're real.

For the practitioners of the ancient tradition, Chicomoztoc is the inner cave that communicates with the exterior through seven portals known as Totonalcayo. That is to say that the cave refers to our inner being, which communicates with the outside world through these portals that are the Mexican equivalent of the world famous chakras.

For the ancient Mexicans, these focal points had colors, names and functions somewhat different from those known as chakras:

a) The first one is named Colotl, which means scorpion. It's located in the sacrum, its color is black and it represents ancestral patterns and our old winds (the energy that we carry from previous lives and ancestors and that the world now knows as Karma).

b) The second one, known as Ihuitl, means feather and is located in our sexual area, the place where the creation of our existence begins. Therefore, if we want it to be benevolent, it should be as light as a feather.

c) The third center is called Pantli, which means flag (the symbol used in the codices to represent number 20). There are 20 glyphs in the calendar and they signify the virtues and challenges that we must face by being born.

d) The fourth one, also known as Xochitl, is located in our chest. It symbolizes the energetic point where we can open ourselves to illumination, which was known by the ancients as flowering.

e) The fifth one is located in our throat and called Topilli, the staff of command, the center of power where our failures reside, but also the possibility of overcoming them in order to reach for the pure power of our words.

f) The sixth one is on our forehead. It's called Chalchiuhuitl, or jade, the most precious mineral for the ancient Mexicans, which symbolizes our full potential, the sacred place where we can be both awake and asleep at the same time, the tonal and the nahual, and enter into dream state (conscious dreams or lucid dreams are those in charge of molding our reality).

g) The seventh one is located in the skullcap and called Tecpatl, or flint. It represents the knives of justice, energetic structures that are found on our head and that give us talents, but also our biggest problems.

For present day practitioners of the Mexican or Toltec teachings, activating these seven centers through the sacred knowledge of what is known as Quetzalcoatl (the Precious Serpent that rises) is to activate the Chicomoztoc or the Cave of Power, something known in other regions of the world by the name of Kundalini.

Finally, the Caves of Power refer also to the ancient training carried out by many of the Eagle, Jaguar, and Serpent Warriors, as well as the Tlamacazquis or Priests, and Rulers, to fully gain access to their power.

Part of the information that is kept about these trainings explains how they consisted. For example, in using caves with a hole in the ceiling, this made it possible for light to filter into darkness.

A thing done in antiquity, and that continues to be done today by the practitioners of the Toltec teachings, is to bring light to each of the centers described above, but in the opposite direction, starting with the skullcap, removing all the old winds or things that you repeat and that make you suffer, healing emotions and opening your perception to lucid dreams and reverie in the forehead, healing and overcoming your wounds and opening yourself to power, beginning to bring energy for your flowering or illumination of your chest, overcoming the astrological challenges that you've been given by birth in order to change them to the grandiose destination that corresponds to you according to your date of birth, lightening your creations so you can perform the reverse process of raising the snake in the Quetzalcoatl, and finally healing the ancestors in the coccyx or sacrum.

There are many other caves of power that we can explore. These ones are only the tip of the iceberg with which I invite you to discover the true Treasure of Mexico, which isn't its gold, but its wisdom.

About the Author:

Sergio Magaña (Ocelocoyotl) author of "Caves of Power Ancient Energy Techniques for Healing, Rejuvenation and Manifestation" is a famous Mexican healer who has been initiated into the 5,000-year-old Toltec lineage of nahualism and the Tol lineage of dreaming knowledge. He has been appointed head of a prestigious project with Club UNESCO for the Protection of Intangible Heritage of Ancient Civilizations.[]

THE 'X' CHRONICLES NEWSPAPER IS AVAILABLE WITH OUR COMPLIMENTS AT
www.xchroniclesnewspaper.com

Published Monthly And Read On-line or Downloaded in more than 7,238 Cities Worldwide.
www.xchroniclesnewspaper.com

Online Shamanic Classes

ONLINE SHAMANIC CLASSES!

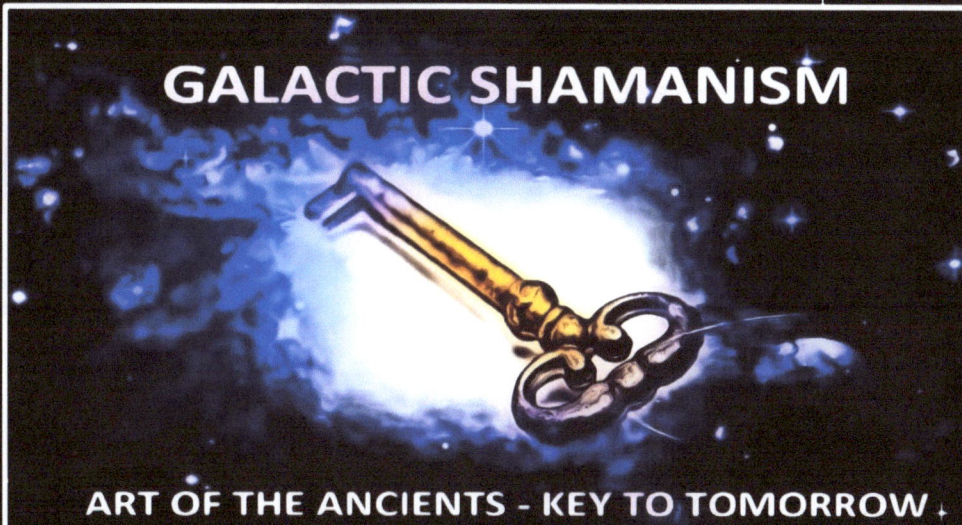

GALACTIC SHAMANISM
ART OF THE ANCIENTS - KEY TO TOMORROW

While shamanism is often seen as an earth based, magical, mystical modality, there is a galactic form firmly rooted in scientific principles.

What if this ancient form can empower you to take charge of your life? What if your entire family could be enfolded and supported by life itself, finding safe passage through turbulent times?

Through this ancient shamanic method, you can manage matter at the quantum level, change outcome and manifest the life you want.

"GALACTIC SHAMANISM: ART OF THE ANCIENTS - KEY TO TOMORROW" is an upcoming series of leading edge, online, affordable classes, designed to guide and support you and your family during these times of transition.

COMING SOON! The first six online classes entitled "OF EARTH" includes:

Class 1: The Medicine Wheel

Class 2: Lower World Shamanic Journey

Class 3: Sanctuary: Creating Sacred Space

Class 4: Power Animals: The Shamanic Art of Shape Shifting

Class 5: Elementals & Faery Folk

Class 6: Omenology

Embrace the magic, empower your life. Study Galactic Shamanism today at
www.findyourpathhome.com/classes

Class curriculum designer and instructor: Gwilda Wiyaka

Certified Shamanic practitioner/ instructor, founder and director of Path Home Shamanic Arts School, with more than 40 years' experience in shamanism from numerous traditions. Gwilda is a preceptor for the University of Colorado School of Medicine, Consultant for Shamanic Affairs at REL-MAR McConnell Media Company and the host of The Science of Magic Radio Show

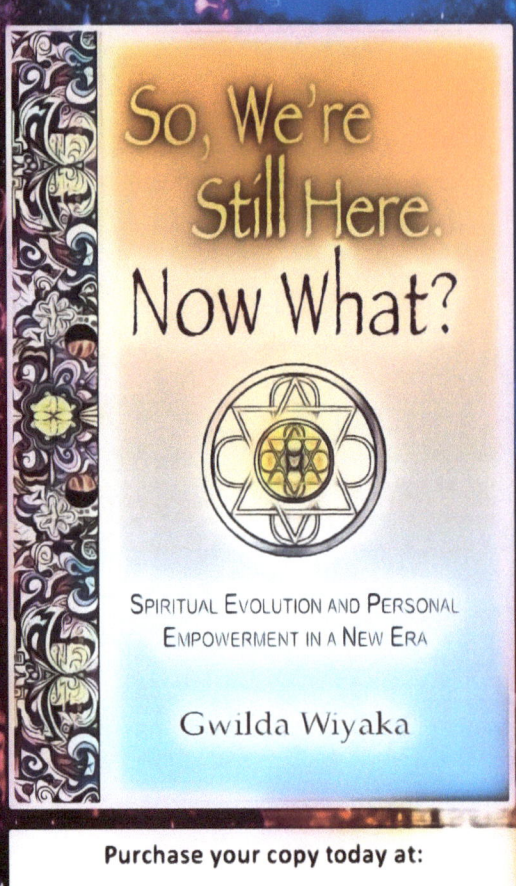

Having the Courage to Tell Our Stories

Diana Raab, PhD

Whether we're affected by change, loss, or pain, finding the time and courage to write can support the healing process. Being fearless and able to take risks is essential for being a good writer. When our fears are released, we accept what happens in our lives, and a sense of wonder can follow.

One of the first things my beloved father-in-law, Alexander, told me just after my breast-cancer diagnosis in 2001 was, "Diana, have no fear." Most of us offer words of wisdom based on our own experiences, and as someone who escaped the Nazis during World War II and emigrated to Canada to start anew, Alexander could have definitely been called a fearless man. Therefore, I took his advice seriously, and it has served me well in many areas of my life. As Ernest Hemingway once said, "There is nothing to writing. All you have to do is sit down at a typewriter and bleed." That was the way I felt when writing my two memoirs, Regina's Closet: Finding My Grandmother's Secret Journal and Healing with Words: A Writer's Cancer Journey. It took a lot of courage to expose my inner self, the voice of my heart, and the feelings of my soul.

Writing takes a huge amount of courage, but submitting work for publication takes even more. If we choose to share our writing, the rewards from taking risks and being courageous is having others read and enjoy what we've written. Some writers would say that if we do not experience fear when telling our personal stories, then we're not really telling the stories we need to tell.

Most writers write because they have to. Writing is where they find their bliss. Sometimes a person might start out wanting to be a writer, but then choose another path for increased financial gain, only to return to writing in later years.

When we're hesitant to write about a particular aspect of our lives, it might be a good idea to stop and think about the reason why. Sometimes we may not be fearful until something happens to trigger those fears. For some people, feeling apprehensive is akin to experiencing a crash landing in a plane. Others might have butterflies in their stomachs, while some might simply get clammy hands.

Writer John Steinbeck said that he was often overcome by terror and shyness and suffered from the fear of writing down his first line. Many writers fear that first sentence, but in my own case, those initial words have always been something I've looked forward to. My first lines are launching pads for the rest of my essay, book, or poem. They actually direct my way of thinking and the trajectory of my writing. The pages of my journal have many first lines that I use in subsequent work—no matter the genre.

There is no doubt that writing, especially personal writing, takes a huge amount of courage. One of my favorite books is The Courage to Create by humanist psychologist Rollo May. He said that courage is not a virtue, but the foundation needed for all other virtues. He claimed that courage makes being and becoming possible. To be courageous, we must make choices that ultimately lead to transformation and bliss. In order for transformation to occur, we must allow our inner selves to become exposed. As May says, it is much easier to be naked physically than it is to become naked psychologically or spiritually, but the latter is necessary in order for deep emotional truths to be revealed in the course of our writing.

Fear can be immobilizing and limit our joy and bliss. If we're fearful, then we're not living in the moment. Living fearlessly can take our feelings to a more peaceful and grounded place. When we consider our fear, it's wise to think about whether it's based on fact or something we've imagined. Sometimes our minds can be very powerful in choosing our direction . . . or lack of it.

Tips for Being Fearless and Gaining Courage When Writing:
- Choose a time of day to write when feeling the most productive.
- Establish calming prewriting rituals.
- Speak to, and spend time with, other writers.
- Take a writing workshop.
- Journal fifteen to twenty minutes a day.
- Write letters.
- Read the work of writers with courage, such as Marcel Rita Dove, and Edmund White.

Gaining the courage to write occurs over time, but it also can happen when we read the work of other fearless writers. One reason why Anaïs Nin has been such a huge influence on my own writing was her transparency, and her ability to express her deepest sentiments without focusing on what others thought about what she wrote. She completely let her guard down during the writing process, and that type of creative liberation is immensely important in order to write with true courage.

About the Author:

Diana Raab, PhD is an award-winning memoirist, poet, blogger, and speaker who advocates the healing and transformative powers of writing. She's the author of eight books and her essays and poetry have been widely published. She's a regular blogger for Psychology Today. Writing for Bliss: Telling Your Story and Transforming Your Life is her ninth book. Website, www.dianaraab.com; https://www.facebook.com/DianaRaab.Author/

Living Creatively with Nature

Kirby Hancock

This article is inspired by personal adventures in the wilderness. It pursues the idea that a simple, well-crafted space has the potential to deepen awareness, improve wellbeing and connect us to the invisible forces of nature in which we live. A space, if constructed properly, benefits the human mind, body, and spirit, by encompassing minds with a stillness of purpose, nourishment of the body, and enticement of the spirit to mythical heights.

Propelled by the momentum of the industrial revolution, human beings spend the majority of time in buildings, with unlimited information and one click shopping ready at the touch of a button. While there are many comforts to be found living in a built environment, it is still a relatively new human adaptation to have drinking water appear at the turn of a lever, or lights turn on at the flip of a switch. In addition, the exponential development of technologies has rapidly changed the way we live, to the point where technological advancements are occurring so quickly, it seems like human evolution is still trying to keep up.

The human dependence on nature may be linked to humanity's survival and wellbeing, more than most people are willing to acknowledge. Ecosystems are operating outside the awareness of most contemporary lifestyles, rendering them as unimportant. This can be problematic, as E.O. Wilson states; "If all of mankind were to disappear, the world would regenerate back to the rich state of equilibrium that existed ten thousand years ago. If insects were to vanish, the environment would collapse into chaos."

A reflection of the present human condition is shown within the condition of nature. Dependence of human survival relies heavily on a maintaining a supportive environment. Wilson continues to suggest, "Nature holds the key to our aesthetic, intellectual, cognitive and even spiritual satisfaction." When the human connection with nature is lost, a piece of humanity is lost. The human ability to find contentment within the embodiment of nature has transformed as rapidly as the human developments of the industrial age.

Science is only beginning to measure the totality in which nature impacts humanity. The term "ecological unconscious," as described by Theodore Roszak, suggests that humans have a psychic dependence on nature. Humanity has depended on nature for the sustenance to survive throughout its existence. The evolution of human survival has depended on a deep connection to nature's rhythms.

When disrupted, the imbalance in nature may manifest as a parallel to disorders within human conditions. Large scale destruction of the environment has become a suicidal tendency among contemporary civilizations.

Acknowledging that nature has an influence on humans beyond physical limitations may be the first step to reconnecting with the elements of nature.

At times, the world of technology can feel like a burden to the human spirit, so it's important to find ways that counterbalance those feelings and find grounded relief. Taking an adventure into the wilderness is one way to do this. Allow time to unplug and reconnect to the intricacies of nature and the natural elements of stone, wood, water, air and fire.

Journeys into the wilderness have been a part of humanity throughout its existence. Motives for such wanderings have links to human survival, outward exploration, recreation, art and spiritual enlightenment. Those motives can be found in nearly every culture at one time or another, and still resonate today.

Acknowledging the powerful influence of nature in our own creative process, my significant other and I embarked on our own wilderness journey. It taught us that in nature, nothing is lost, only transformed. By connecting deeper to ourselves and the unseen mysteries around us, we were transformed.

High into the Montana mountains we went, leaving behind our daily lives with its routines and responsibilities, to follow the wisdom of place. Weaving through trees, one step at a time, we followed the paths left by the four-legged ones, such as deer, moose, coyote, bear, elk, and wolves. Our self-ignited ceremony had begun.

We stopped. We listened with our ears, eyes, nose, skin, intuition, feeling and imagination, to the current of a pristine mountain snowmelt as it made its journey towards the ocean. In this way, the flow of water circulates endlessly from the heavens, to the land, and back to the ocean. Connecting us to its journey. Quenching a thirst beyond hydration.

Along the way, the appearance of stone markers emerged from the land, speaking to us in the symbolic grammar of the natural environment. Appearing here of its own accord, this self-manifestation of nature can be said to be a spontaneous eruption of the divine.

To evoke a greater understanding of the qualities of water and stone, we chose to create our own space to form a steam sweat. Traditions of steam sweats date back tens of thousands of years, and evidence can be found across the world in different shapes and forms. Although we both had previously experienced traditional Native American sweat lodges, this was not a re-creation of anything we had been in before, but rather a creative exercise to try something new. A blown down tree served as the root of our adventure in creating a space for steam.

The purpose of sweats has traditionally been to purify the body, mind and spirit, so that a new sense of Self and connection to the divine may manifest. It involves the elements of earth, water, air and fire, to connect the physical world with the nonphysical realm.

The choreography of creating our steam space involved using only the materials available to us in the forest. As wanderers of Montana's Wilds, we relied on the gifts found around us, as there is always more to the forest than what we think we see. Tree limbs and pieces of dead wood were used to shape the height and width of the space of our sweat.

(Continued on Page 33)

Living Creatively with Nature

Living Creatively with Nature

Continued from Page 33

We gathered stones to heat, water to pour and wood to burn. It became a ritual of seeing, doing, being, allowing. We created a sacred mound with an elk bone and deer antlers found along our journey, to connect us to the animal spirits. We created fire to heat our souls and illuminate our hearts. We gathered some good ol' Montana sage, rolled into balls and placed on a tray of pine bark to burn, in order to purify ourselves and cleanse the layers of feelings and emotions that create separateness in our modern world. This brought us more into balance with ourselves, each other, and the natural life around us.

The simple act of collecting stones has a way of grounding our attention closer to the earth. Once the stones are heated and removed from the fire, poured water sizzles, spats and bubbles over the rocks, creating the wet, hot atmosphere, unleashing the imagination, dreams and emotions up to the stars. With intention, we would breathe the steam into our bodies and release our prayers to the heavens above. We continued this until the stones were cooled from the water, no longer glowing red as they had moments earlier.

Sensing something was different in the forest on the cool autumn night, elk were drawn to take a look the sweat as well. This made us realize that we are not so separate from the elk. As creatures on Earth, we all have a primal yearning to explore the curiosities of the world around us.

The next morning, we returned to the cold stones and cooled ashes of charred wood. It was a moment to be still, reflect, and share our visions from the steam filled experience. While staring into the void of chilly morning darkness, we imagined how we can bring the wildness of such a journey into our home of "domestic" life.

So, we decided to take our curiosity home to become a regular part of our daily lives, transforming an old cement slab in the yard where a tool shed had once been, into a natural building that can harness the power of steam to improve wellbeing. The need for a personal sauna to lounge, love and laugh was realized. We re-created our adventure from the mountains in a new form at our Bozeman home with a Finnish style sweat. It has become a sacred space to us, that physically, mentally and spiritually alters us and renews us from the mundane.

In the few steps taken from the house to the sauna, there is a sensory realignment. Feeling the crunch of snow between the toes, an autumn breeze on our skin, the soft summer grass beneath our feet, and getting a glimpse at the changing light patterns, remind us of the season's influence that is always around us.

The process of sauna is meditative. We slow down. The sound of the steam on the rocks dances in our ears. The smell of cedar calms our mind and the warmth seeps deep into our bodies. We listen, we think, we feel. A space made of natural elements has a way of soothing the senses.

We named our sauna Kilkipoana, the Finnish word for Turtle. A space designed for going inward. Representing our need to slow down and follow a peaceful path. Forming a sanctuary to unplug from the phone and computer, and focus on our breath. Indeed, the sauna ignites the lost art of being present in the moment.

We are living in an unprecedented time where it's easy to become focused on the latest trends and alternative facts. Those are temporary.

Connect with something timeless. Listen to wind in the trees. Float down a river. However you connect to the elements, follow the spark and let it ignite your own fire within.

About the Author:
Kirby Hancock is an architectural designer, avid outdoorsman, craftsman and founder of Transformative Ecologies, LLC. Years of building experience shaped his pursuit for healthier buildings, structures and designs that positively support the human experience and connection with the physical world. His work serves the needs of people and communities by fusing human emotions and experiences with the use of natural building materials, holistic design and engagement with the natural world. Inspired by the mountains and rivers of Montana, he enjoys exploring wild places with his significant other and their energetic bird dog.
Website: www.transformativeecologies.com
Email: kirbyh@transformativeecologies.com
Phone: 406.589.6957 []

Color Meanings and Psychology

Red Color Meaning – The color of passion and drama. This color attracts the most attention and is associated with strong emotions such as love and anger. Red is the color used universally to signify danger, courage, strength, and power. Red is stimulating, vibrant and exciting. Red inspires desire with a strong link to sexuality and increased appetites. In Chinese culture red represents luck and prosperity. Use red when you want to get pulses racing and to inspire action. However, use carefully as red can evoke feelings of aggression and cause visual strain.

Orange Color Meaning – The color of encouragement. The combination of yellow and red makes orange convey excitement, warmth and enthusiasm. Social and inviting, this is the color of the extrovert, exuding happiness and joy, releasing inhibitions. Need to be inspired into action or have a positive outlook on life? Orange is a motivating and encouraging color. Orange is appealing to young people. It stimulates the appetite and is associated with healthy good. However, the negative connotations of orange include insincerity, exhibitionism and self indulgence.

Yellow Color Meaning – The color of optimism. Yellow is a compelling color that conveys youthful, fresh energy. This color of sunshine is uplifting and illuminating and associated with success and confidence. Yellow stimulates the left side of the brain, helping with clear thinking and quick decision making. Yellow grabs attention because the eye sees yellow first. The downside of yellow is that it can induce anxiety and cause one to be over-critical. It also signifies cowardice.

Yellow Color Meaning – The color of optimism. Yellow is a compelling color that conveys youthful, fresh energy. This color of sunshine is uplifting and illuminating and associated with success and confidence. Yellow stimulates the left side of the brain, helping with clear thinking and quick decision making. Yellow grabs attention because the eye sees yellow first. The downside of yellow is that it can induce anxiety and cause one to be over-critical. It also signifies cowardice.

Find Your Path Home

Shamanic Healing is the Key To Personal Empowerment and Spiritual Evolution!

All four levels of our being: physical, emotional, mental and spiritual, must be addressed in order for us to enjoy balanced, healthy, abundant lives. Shamanism is a spiritual healing modality that has been around 50,000 years and practiced by healers of nearly every indigenous culture.

To find quality shamanic healing you can trust, regardless of where you live, you need look no further than Find Your Path Home Long Distance Shamanic Healing Program.

All Path Home Long Distance Healing practitioners have been trained and certified through the Path Home Shamanic Arts School, a Colorado State Certified Occupational School. They have been handpicked and personally trained by Founder/Director Gwilda Wiyaka to uphold the excellence of Find Your Path Home's Long Distance Program.

Change your life. Live abundantly. Schedule a long distance shamanic healing session with Gwilda Wiyaka or one of her quality practitioners today.

Call 303-775-3431
Visit: http://findyourpathhome.com/shamanic-healing-sessions
Email: touchin@findyourpathhome.com

Transform the Past with Easy Techniques!

Maureen Higgins, MA

Everyone has a past with good memories and difficult memories. You are born into an ancestry with good memories and difficult memories, which are also something you carry. Some memories can keep bothering you, even if it's been years since they occurred. Some may even be unconscious and act as a sabotage, keeping you from receiving the very things you want in your life.

Before you were born, your soul decided what you wanted to learn in your lifetime and who you wanted to learn these things with. Some souls are in your "soul group," meaning you have spent all your lifetimes together, like a troupe of actors and actresses picking a theme to act and deciding who are going to play the parts. Someone in the soul group will be the hero; some will act as spirit guides; some will be very difficult lesson-givers, and anything in between. We take turns with these roles to see what they are like, while learning love and compassion along the way.

Together, your soul group looks at all the lifetimes you've had unresolved challenges in, to see which themes still need some learning. You then pick an ancestry to fit this theme. Some of the ancestors are soul group members; others are close souls who have been in many of the lifetimes with you, but not all of them.

The lifetimes and ancestry that fit the theme are around you, much like an astrology chart influencing who you are and what you think and feel, since everyone is interconnected through a giant matrix connecting everybody together.

How do you affect change for yourself when there are so many influences around you from these different lifetimes and your ancestry? Start thinking, "Oneness."

Everybody and everything is One. If you put the spirit of everybody and everything together, it makes up the Oneness field, or Source.

All of us as One decided to have all of these experiences together, to see what it was like in a variety of different bodies, from the vibration of hate (Dimension 1) all the way to the vibration of love (Dimension 11). What is it like to experience an existence that's all about hate? What's it like to experience an existence that's all about love, and anything in between? We on planet earth are around Dimensions 3 to 4.

We, as a Oneness field, had decided we'd experience the lower dimension realities for a set period of time. We decided that, when the time was right, we'd give ourselves tools to work our way through these themes we've chosen to experience, so we can move to a higher vibration more aligned with love. Now is the time.

A big way to help shift the collective to a higher consciousness is to work on yourself. We are connected to everybody and everything, so it automatically heals your ancestry, other lifetimes and the collective. We can also intentionally offer the healing to those around us, defaulting how the work helps according to everyone's spirit or Higher Self.

An extremely effective tool that helps your ancestors, all the lifetimes you're in, and the collective, is to "cross over" lost souls. This simple act of crossing others over is huge, since everyone alive can feel the grief, pain and unresolved issues of the person who hasn't crossed over. Once someone has crossed over, you will feel lighter and more peaceful. This technique is good to do regularly, since there are many souls that need this kind of assistance.

A common reason people don't cross is due to not wanting to leave someone behind, and not realizing they can come back to visit loved ones once they cross over. Some people are afraid to see people who have already died, due to difficulties they had with them while they were alive. Some people believe in heaven and hell and don't think they did a good enough job while on earth, so they are afraid they may end up in hell.

You can follow this script to help cross lost souls to their next highest level destination – a peaceful, loving place.

- I ask to pinpoint all lost souls.
- I ask to encircle them in a bubble of loving crystalline energy, which is all about love.
- I ask that a tunnel of light appears with any loved ones and spirit guides to cross them over with the perpetual message that all is forgiven, there is only love, and a loving place to go to. Any hell is self-created, or a belief on earth that isn't true. There is only one place for everyone to go, which is all about love. You don't need to see anyone on the other side that you don't want to see, but you'll find that everybody loves you and no one is concerned about this lifetime anymore. You can come back to see anyone who is left behind once you cross, and you'll find that you'll be more helpful, since the tunnel of light will cleanse away all the worries and problems from this life, and leave you with love and wisdom to share once you go back to visit your loved ones. We ask that the highest level guides ensure that all souls have crossed over.

Another simple technique – ask to disconnect, delete, splice out and transform your energy field from your ancestors and all lifetimes influencing you, from the issues, patterns, beliefs, memories, emotions and behaviors not serving you. Ask that you reconnect with full resolution and love. Also ask that you bring in the exact opposite energy of the issue so that you can delete, splice out and transform the issues, patterns, beliefs, memories, emotions and behaviors, down to the smallest particle of energy level.

Due to this era of great change, we are shifting so quickly that we all need to work on ourselves regularly. Find a practice that works for you and stick to it. You are the change the world seeks.

About the Author:

Maureen Higgins, MA founded Wings of Freedom as an alternative counseling business in 1998. She has developed numerous healing systems, including putting many of her techniques on audios. She found that her clients could use a healing often, which isn't affordable or practical, and decided to record healing audios, set up like a healing session, so they could play these audios daily to keep the healing going and continue making rapid progress. She now offers them to the public on her website www.wingsoffreedom1.com. Maureen teaches workshops and offers teacher training programs on her many healing techniques, and offers a service called "3 Questions" to help give intuitive direction during times of change (also listed on her website).

Silence and the Unitive Experience

Christina Donnell, Ph.D.

There is an unseemly coarseness and tumult to our times which robs the grace from the fabric of our interrelatedness. At first, it sounds completely naïve to suggest that now might be the time to embark on the ancient journey from separation to union, the journey from our own Self back to a state of Oneness. Yet that is exactly the claim that this article explores. It is a call to a deeper spiritual consciousness, by which awareness becomes 'centerless' and the dichotomy of I-Other is transcended.

Much of what is noisy about our times is that we are beholden to surface reality – Facebook, Twitter, news feeds, texting, busy daily life. Abandoning the surface of things takes something more than curiosity or a need for depth or solitude. It is to risk being moved – moved from the person we were to the person we may become.

The development of the unitive experience (or non-dual awareness) requires us to abandon surface impressions and patterns, to abandon what has become comfortable and to embrace a depth of being that asks us to enter that which is wholly unknown – the depths and dimensions of silence. Silence was here before anything else, and it resides inside and around all things. It is the most primary phenomenon in existence and is the home of union.

Our body has an innate capacity for apprehending the Absolute and experiencing union. There is a palpable silence which is a substance – textured and layered, permeating every cell of our body. As we enter the mystery of silence, its presence resonates throughout the fibers of our flesh, extending inwardly, and is connected to the same silence of the cosmos outwardly. Our body is the necessary meeting point where the inward stillness meets up with the immense silence of the cosmos, and the unitive experience is born. Upon entering the great layers and folds of the substance of silence, the infinite appears of its own accord inside the body, and consciousness of it may be stabilized, enriched, and defined. When we find the entry into this vast stillness, our lives are irrevocably changed and a monumental transition takes place.

I consider the emergence of non-dual awareness an organic development. It is an interior process, disclosing what is already present inside us, rather than setting out on a path looking for something new. There is only attention and its awakening. New capacities emerge by developing dimensions of attention that go beyond usual awareness. Silence must be entered, and one must deeply participate. Participation in the silence is the remaking of the consciousness. From here, the body's innate perceptual gift emerges.

So, if we are going to explore unity consciousness, we simply can't leave out the medium in which union emerges. Silence is its medium, as the painter's medium is color and the musician's medium is sound. In the development of unity consciousness, the medium is silence, and it is a reservoir to which we may endlessly return. There we are privileged to drink as often and deeply as we desire. Unity consciousness is indeed an organic process, and I refer to the phases of development as The Gathering, The Stillness, and The Surrender. Respectively, each denotes reaching deeper layers of the silence and greater interior changes.

The Gathering

The first phase requires quieting the surface consciousness – thoughts, images, emotions. It lifts you to a new level of perception whereby a new inflow of life is received.

Silence is a kind of touch. To be fully with silence requires that we develop a capacity to be present to both the subtlest qualities of its touch and to the way this touch resonates our interiority. When silence announces itself, you have begun to find the way out of separation consciousness. It is the most difficult phase, because most of our attention is allocated to surface consciousness.

The Stillness

In the second phase, attention passes to a state characterized by intense stillness, in which it rests in that reality to which it yet dares not surrender. When one comes to this point, the brain becomes very still – yet, it is highly sensitive, vigorous, fully alive. Will and imagination are silenced, bringing a state of emptiness. In this state of emptiness, there is a sense of a mind that has penetrated its unknown depths. The difficult terrain of emptiness is truly the fertile soil of change, yet it is deeply alarming and hard to trust, because the conditioning of everything you know so well is essentially dying into another plane of consciousness.

The surface mind begins to surrender the strings of reality, allowing consciousness to sink into the stillness and silence from which the Absolute appears – where everything is nurtured into existence at every moment. These you are participatory with, within the Silence. Experiences of passive union begin to occur in this phase.

The Surrender

In the third phase, one soaks in the silence and energizes oneself on those high levels of energy from a deeper reality, which are dark to the intellect, but radiant to the heart. It is a manifestation of that indivisible power of a different kind of knowing through unity. One surrenders into the deepest layers of the silence and is merged within it. When the larger reality appears, it is given to us and we know it, as we cannot know it by the ordinary devices of thought.

There is a turning of attention from the world of multiplicity, with which the intelligence is accustomed and able to deal, towards new powers of perception, which we never knew we possessed. Instead of sharply perceiving the fragment, we apprehend, yet know not how, the solemn presence of the whole. This awareness is balanced by a great ongoing sense of expansion, of new worlds made ours, as we receive the inflow of its life. This revealed reality is apprehended by way of participation, not by observation. And this experience of the "Whole" seems to be given, rather than attained.

In withdrawal from the busy, surface consciousness, One sinks down to the ground of Being and the apparent Universe. Our Being experiences the 'Substance of All that Is.' Multiplicity is resolved into Unity, a unity with which the perceiving self is merged. Here, there is an enhancement of vitality, equanimity, and joy.

This incredible eternity is stamped into the core of our being. When our awareness and attention can touch here, a different way of existing and serving in our world unfolds. The Self is lifted to another plane of consciousness and becomes an agent of the Absolute—an energizing center. Sometimes I liken it to a destiny of incarnating the eternal in time. For this, we humans are made. One simply needs to bring awareness down into every cell of the body, remain quiet there, and meet the silence. You cannot understand it. There is only to be it. Until you have tasted the degree of this inner fulfillment, you hardly dare dream that it is possible. This fulfillment gets deeper and deeper, more and more complete; and you know with a certainty that is born of experience. We can slip into unity consciousness with the same ease as we slip into the seamless embrace of water. Something very ancient, eternal within us, already trusts that this embrace will hold us. The source of these living waters is stamped in the very core of our being. It is the Substance of All that Is.

About the Author:

Christina Donnell, Ph.D. is the Director of the Winds of Change Association, an educational organization dedicated to offering programs that tend our evolving consciousness. Christina is a natural born, pragmatic mystic, spiritual teacher and public speaker. She is the author of the award-winning book, Transcendent Dreaming: Stepping Into Our Human Potential. Her latest offering is the Unitive Life audio series which is a rich foray into silence and the emergence of non-dual awareness. Her website: www.christinadonnell.com []

Of Earth and Sky

Resonance

Cody Alexander

Within the hustle and stress of daily life, it is easy to forget we are children of the cosmos. As such, we cannot help but be affected by planetary shifts and the vagaries of stellar events.

How much are we influenced by the movements of earth and sky?

As a shamanic practitioner, I have observed subjective responses in others that appear to coincide with solar and seismic changes. Along with my own experiences, reports from clients and friends over a period of years align with documented research that we may be more sensitive to these changes than we thought.

Hours to days prior to or during a large earthquake occurring somewhere on the globe, many have experienced sudden feelings of dizziness, being ungrounded, anxiety, a dark sense of imminence, or disorientation. Is it possible we are so sensitive to the movements of the earth, that the shifting of our planet hundreds of miles away registers in the body? Strong stellar changes appear to similarly affect us. Solar flares, solar wind, geomagnetic storms, eclipses, notable planetary and interstellar alignments, etc., may not only coincide with geophysical events, but with personal reports of a wide variety of symptoms, including extreme agitation, heightened emotional sensitivity, the appearance of sunburn without sun exposure, dizziness, memory loss, confusion, a feeling of being outside of space and time.

From a shamanic viewpoint, it could be argued that fluctuating energy/frequencies of the earth and sun are putting increasing pressure on the physical, emotional, mental and spiritual (or energetic) body of each individual. This increase in frequency puts pressure on any restrictions, bringing to the surface those places where we carry historical damage. Could this be related to instances of violent release in some who are already so compromised that any additional discomfort pushes them over the edge?

Bartenders, police officers and emergency workers can attest to the increase in incidents and intensity of conflict during the full moon.

In tracking solar and earth events for years, I have traced their relationship not only to personal shifts and crises, but those of friends, family and clients. There is enough coincidental correlation to warrant a deeper look at our interaction with the earth – our home – and the universe.

Research indicates that changes in the magnetic field of the sun directly impact the earth with varying effects. Solar and terrestrial events seem to be linked, solar events resulting in terrestrial geomagnetic reactions, and producing a wide range of measurable responses in humans. According to environmental scientist Neil Cherry, many studies have shown "significant physical, biological and health effects that are associated with changes in Solar and Geomagnetic Activity (S-GMA)."

Also notable are apparent changes in the light of our own star, particularly over the past decade. Living in an environment devoid of pollution, shifts in the visible spectrum can be remarkable. There are days when the light is so intense at my home in the mountains, it appears blue-white instead of the warm yellow normally associated with the sun. This phenomenon might be disregarded as a visual idiosyncrasy, an aspect of weather or place, were it not also noted by others in various locations.

One such day occurred on March 19th, 2018 where I live in the southern mountains of Colorado. The light was such an extreme halogen blue-white then and for days afterward, that I traced the date to NASA's Spaceweather website. I uncovered the following report:
"On March 18th, a crack opened in Earth's magnetic field. Solar wind poured in, fueling a moderately strong (G2-class) geomagnetic storm… an unusually-wide stream of solar wind [has been blowing] around our planet. Literally, the geomagnetic field has been shaking back and forth. 'Magnetic activity has been relatively high since March 14th… Magnetometers all around the world are registering this.'"

Accompanying graphs delineate impressive data on the resulting shifts in the earth's magnetic field as a result of the solar storm.

Are we, too, energetically "shaking back and forth"? Is the visible/invisible spectrum affected by intense solar activity?

One NASA article, discussing a recent discovery about how the solar magnetic field is generated, notes:

"…powerful eruptions on the Sun's surface can disrupt electronic systems on Earth such as GPS, satellites, radio communications, and electrical power grids, and create space weather than can potentially change weather patterns on Earth."

We are electrical beings. Beyond the physical effect on our equipment, how many of us alter our mood for better or worse, simply dependent upon whether there are clouds or the sky is clear? Perhaps our reactions are merely a subjective response, but is there a deeper influence as a result of solar fluctuations?

We are bathed in the light of our sun, periodically blasted by energy from solar activity, resulting in mild to extreme terran effects as evidenced above. Science notes that the effects can range from negligible to catastrophic, purely according to the directional relationship between a solar occurrence and the position of the earth.

What happens if an event occurs on the side of the sun facing away from us? Does the entire solar electromagnetic field shift in relation to its own violent changes? No matter how much time the physical movement of a solar wave is reported to take on its journey to, through, and beyond our planet, is it possible that we are immediately affected, as the electromagnetic field of the sun and that of the earth interact? Or does the current scientific, linear view on the position of the solar event relative to the earth hold true – that the variance in intensity is determined by whether or not we are in its direct path? Subjective reports indicate that, for some of us, the effect is immediate.

What about the earth? Before, during and after geomagnetic activity, does the planet's electromagnetic field shift as a result? Given the human body has an electromagnetic field just as the sun and earth, how close do we have to be to register a physical, emotional, mental or spiritual (energetic) response?

Ultimately, we are connected to all that is. When viewed through the lens of "oneness," there is no mystery as to our reaction to stellar and earth events, regardless of the illusion of distance or separation.

As a resource for those interested in tracking solar and terran activity, solar information is available on the Spaceweather site www.spaceweather.com, and the global earthquake map is at https://earthquake.usgs.gov/.
To share your observations, email: earthsky365@gmail.com

About the Author: Cody Alexander is a Path Home Shamanic Arts School certified shamanic practitioner and instructor with over ten years of experience in shamanic work, and more than thirty years of study in practical application of esoteric concepts and spiritual/energetic healing. Cody created North Shield, a CD of original prayer songs, and co-created The Winds of Time, a transformational and evolutionary musical CD, with fellow artist Gwilda Wiyaka. She is an author, editor, composer and storyteller (The Spoken Wheel Storytelling Troupe). Her website: www.codyalexander.net.

Welcome To SimulTV

SimulTV Lite

Up To 70 **American Channels** and 100's of **Movies On Demand** all for **$6.99 per Month.**

INCLUDING EXCLUSIVE CHANNELS LIKE XZONE, SCI-FI, HORROR AND MUCH MORE

EXCLUSIVE LIVE EVENTS
OCT 25 - NOV 3

We also offer our SimulTV Set Top Box or STB at $69 with 4 mo. FREE of SimulTV Lite. It comes with 2 additional accts. for other devices. The STB has over 100 TOP BRAND VIDEO GAMES incl. for a one time charge of $69

www.ingramcontent.com/pod-product-compliance
Lightning Source LLC
Chambersburg PA
CBHW041226040426
42444CB00002B/66